URBAN SCHOOL LEADERSHIP:

ISSUES AND STRATEGIES

Eugene T. W. Sanders

EYE ON EDUCATION
6 Depot Way West, Suite 106
Larchmont, N.Y. 10538

Library of Congress Cataloging-in-Publication Data

Sanders, Eugene T. W. , 1957-
    Urban school leadership: issues and strategies / by Eugene
T. W. Sanders.
        p.   cm.
    Includes bibliographical references (p.) and index.
    ISBN 1-883001-72-2
    1. Urban schools—United States—Administration. 2. Edu-
cation, Urban—Social aspects—United States. 3. School management and organization—United States. 4. Educational leadership—United States I. Title.
LC5131.S25 1999
370' .9173' 2—dc21   98-54127
                                                                      CIP

Production services provided by:
Bookwrights
1211 Courtland Drive
Raleigh, NC 27604

This book is dedicated to my father,
Mr. American Sanders, Sr. (1912-1981), and my mother,
Mrs. Lena M. Sanders
(matriarch of the Sanders family)

MEET THE AUTHOR

Dr. Eugene T. W. Sanders is Chair of the Department of Educational Administration and Supervision and Director of the Doctoral Program in Leadership Studies at Bowling Green State University in Bowling Green, Ohio. He received his Ph.D. in Educational Administration with an emphasis on organizational management from Bowling Green and currently teaches courses in organizational change, staff development, and community relations and politics in educational organizations. He also serves as president of The Institute for Organizational Leadership, a human resource consulting firm.

Dr. Sanders is a former teacher and school administrator in Ohio. He currently serves as Executive Regional Secretary for the Northwest Region of the Ohio School Boards Association. He is a member of the American Association of School Administrators and the National Association of Professors of Educational Administration.

Dr. Sanders' research interests are urban educational leadership and transformational issues associated with traditionally under-represented populations in metropolitan school contexts. Dr. Sanders has made over seventy-five professional presentations at national, regional and state research conferences and is often sought after by school and human resource organizations for staff development and administrative leadership workshops.

ACKNOWLEDGMENTS

This book has been influenced by the recommendations, support, and analysis of several individuals. It became apparent quite early that to write a successful book requires the work of a number of dedicated professionals. First, I would like to thank my research associate of the last nine years, Dr. Karen Patterson-Stewart, president and chief executive officer of Patterson-Stewart Consultant Services, for her review and critique of this work and all of my manuscripts. Second, I would like to thank Brenda Kallio, a doctoral student in Leadership Studies at Bowling Green State University. Ms. Kallio worked numerous extra hours on this project and many of the deadlines would not have been reached without her involvement. Few academic and professional successes would have been possible without the continuing support of my secretary, Mrs. Karen Gerkens. Mrs. "G" is a professional in every sense of the word. Her dedication to the Department of Educational Administration and Supervision at Bowling Green State University and to me is the essence of teamwork and community.

Additional acknowledgment is warranted to Jacquelyn May (Bowling Green Junior High School) and Alicia May (St. Al's Elementary School) and Jennifer May (Rogers High School) for securing numerous research articles from the library and to Judy Maxey and Sherry Haskins for their support in the word processing center at Bowling Green. I also would like to acknowledge the support of my colleagues: Dr. Marcia Salazar-Valentine, Dr. Robert Ludwig, Dr. Patrick Pauken, Dr. David Nicholls, and Dr. Judy Jackson May of the Department of Educational Administration and Supervision at Bowling Green State University and my two mentors, Dr. Patricia Reed and Dr. William York. I would also like to thank Dr. Les Sternberg, Dean of the College of Education and Human Development; Dr. Charles Middleton, Provost and Vice President of Academic Affairs; and Dr. Sidney Ribeau, President, Bowling Green State University; and Dr. Kofi Lomotey, Provost, Medgar Evers College, New York for their support of me and my academic endeavors.

I would also like to thank Judy Alston, Ira Bogotch, Leslie Fenwick, Frank Smith, Donald Walters, and Thomas Williams.

Finally, I owe special thanks to my family: my brothers, American and Michael; and my sisters, Doris, Nettie, Sheila, Carolyn, Patricia, Amy, and Mary. Special thanks go to my brother Bishop Rufus G. W. Sanders and my sister-in-law Dr. JoAnn Sanders of Heidelberg College.

INTRODUCTION

Most school reform efforts within the last fifteen years can be traced to the 1983 publication of *A Nation at Risk*. Terrell Bell, Secretary of Education during publication of the report, was responsible for coordinating the work of the National Commission on Educational Excellence. The essence of this report suggested that America's competitive edge was being limited by the lack of achievement and performance in schools. Since the publication of *A Nation at Risk*, there have been over 150 reports from various organizations that have criticized the efforts of public education. There is agreement among researchers and practitioners that urban schools have been depicted as ineffective and in need of reform.

Urban School Leadership: Issues and Strategies attempts to provide a comprehensive overview of the major leadership issues facing urban schools. Understanding the historical, social, economic, and political context of metropolitan communities is critical in order to appreciate the complexity associated with adequately addressing urban problems. This book also provides practical recommendations for improvement to address what the National Commission on Educational Excellence referred to as the nation's greatest challenge. Urban school reform is directly related to the activities and programs in central cities. The role of government and city development is largely related to the reform efforts in urban education.

In order to address the current status of urban education in America, it is important to examine the current status of American cities. Major shifts in technology, economics, and demographics have been occurring in American cities during the past twenty-five years. Advances in technology have made significant contributions to the organization of work and process in which cities have functioned (Glickman, 1998). These authors suggest that because of the increased freedom promoted by technology, jobs have been relocated from cities to lowest cost markets, which tend to be located in the suburbs. Firms that experience growth in high-technology industries tend to locate in suburbs. The result is that advances in technology ultimately may have a negative impact on the urban community's ability to respond to market changes and to provide sufficient support for students enrolled in urban schools.

Economic change in cities during the last twenty-five years is an important area for school leaders to understand and appreciate. Technology has made it easier for corporations to transcend international markets. As a result, "it [technology] was one of a myriad of factors that helped to disperse economic activities around the globe and profoundly alter the nature of work and urban development" (Wyly, Glickman, and Lahr, 1998, p. 9). The authors noted that the increase of global markets has had a negative impact on urban communities and has led to less economic security.

For most urban communities there has been a growth in the service industry. The authors noted that in 1997, only fifteen percent of Americans (18.6 million workers) had jobs in manufacturing. This percentage is significant because major urban cities that had depended on manufacturing "suffered debilitating employment losses from the decline in this once robust sector" (p. 10). The authors contend that this growth in the service industry has been more helpful to suburban than urban communities. The impact on urban schools is obvious. With a reduced industrial and manufacturing base in urban communities, schools received less financial support and ultimately fewer financial resources for children.

The most obvious shift in urban communities over the last twenty-five years has occurred in demographics. According to Wyly, Glickman, and Lahr (1998), the white population declined from eighty-eight percent to eighty-three percent between 1970 and 1995. The population shifts in the Hispanic population reflected a growth of 10.3 percent during this period. Other significant demographic shifts that are notable for urban communities include a decline in the married population (72 percent to 61 percent), and an increase in the proportion of both divorced and single adults tripled to 9.2 percent. The authors also indicated that less than 20 percent of the population meets the traditional definition of a married couple with children present. Other significant demographic changes include: an increase in urban communities of immigrants, currently at the highest levels since World War II; and the rise of female participation in the labor force. Immigrants tend to select the nation's largest cities for living and working. These changes in demographics suggest that urban schools are faced with the challenge of addressing multiple cultures, languages, and value systems.

Perhaps the most significant implication for urban communities in the last twenty-five years is the impact of income distribution and poverty levels. Between 1960 and 1973, national poverty levels declined by nearly one-half. Urban poverty rates, however, increased dramatically in the 1980s. Even during periods of economic growth, urban communities did not experience substantial increases in income and actually experienced slightly higher levels of poverty during the most prosperous times.

Poverty has the most devastating impact on children. For example, twenty-three percent of all children and forty-six percent of African-American children lived in poverty in 1993 (Blank, 1997). African-Americans (thirty-three percent) and Hispanics (thirty-one percent) experience far higher incidences of poverty than whites (ten percent). Blank noted that poverty remains heavily focused in industrial cities, which are home to nearly half of all poor individuals. Wyly, Glickman, and Lahr (1998) noted "cities losing middle-class families are left with more households in poverty; more single-parent families; declining property values; and underfunded, deteriorating infrastructures and schools" (p. 15).

OVERVIEW OF THE BOOK

During the writing of this book, it became apparent that the magnitude of leadership issues and urban education reform deserved more attention than was possible in this publication. As a result, the goal of this text is to identify key leadership issues in urban schools and provide practical examples and recommendations for addressing these concerns. The book has been divided into three major sections. Chapters one, two and three address contextual variables for urban school leadership. Chapter one introduces readers to the theory of circular hopelessness and its relationship to poverty among urban students. The purpose of this chapter is to inform urban school policymakers about aspects of American culture that result in systemic interactions in urban communities that can create hopelessness in students. Chapter two addresses academic achievement and parental involvement as two of the most significant areas for urban schools and communities. Chapter three addresses the issue of self-esteem in urban children with specific focus on African-American youth.

Chapters four, five, six, and seven identify internal variables necessary for creating successful urban school leaders. These chapters provide examples and recommendations for the key leadership positions in urban education. The collaboration and interaction of these key people are central to the success of urban schools. Chapter four discusses the contemporary urban teacher; chapter five, the urban principal; chapter six, urban superintendency; and chapter seven, the urban school board

Chapters eight, nine, and ten identify external variables that urban school leaders need to be aware to create an effective organization. The purpose of these chapters is to help urban leaders cultivate key external constituencies that will be essential for success in the next century. The focus includes a critical analysis of community relations and politics in urban settings (chapter eight), the need to create effective change strategies (chapter nine) and a futuristic view of leadership challenges for urban schools in the new millennium (chapter ten).

TABLE OF CONTENTS

1

CIRCULAR HOPELESSNESS, POVERTY, AND URBAN SCHOOLS

INTRODUCTION

This chapter offers recommendations for schools and social-service agencies to combat circular hopelessness and provides a theoretical framework for understanding and assisting children of poverty.

The urban school picture often portrays only students of color. In fact, not only are students of color impacted by urban policies, but a substantial number of white students live in and are served by urban school organizations. The common thread that ties all of these students together is their socioeconomic level. Regardless of race, socioeconomic challenges are consistent across all levels of involvement in urban schools.

The traditional American school has assumed a number of tasks that are significantly different from the roles and responsibilities of schools twenty or thirty years ago. These responsibilities have directed the school's attention to a number of social phenomena that impact children such as drugs, crime, violence, and chronic issues of self-esteem and hopelessness. For the first

1

time in a number of years, the public has reported violence, crime, and gang activity as the primary problems for schools. Violence, crime, and gang activity have replaced more traditional public concerns such as discipline, teacher competence, financial management, and alcohol and substance abuse. For many years, the public viewed drug and alcohol abuse as the most significant issues facing schools. All of these concerns have one consistent theme that must be addressed in any discussion of restructuring and change for children in schools and society: the potency of poverty.

Although poverty adversely affects adults with regard to low wages, limited employment opportunities, and family stability, there is perhaps no single group as helpless to change their own position as children who live in low socioeconomic conditions. While the primary focus of this book is concerned with urban education and children, it is significant to note that literature documents that children from urban, rural, as well as suburban communities are affected by poverty. Issues of concern in the literature regarding poverty, children, and school success have been well documented. Issues of the stigma associated with school-lunch programs, assignment to lower tracked classes based on race or socioeconomic status, issues of safety while coming to and from school, and concerns about the quality and quantity of competent professionals who serve in urban school communities are but a few examples of how children of poverty are relegated to lower class status in public schools. Perhaps the most significant and damaging implication impacting poor urban students is the perception of them held by school administrators, teachers, social-service groups, and support staff. They often assume that poor students do not care about school, success in life, and have severely limited abilities to become productive citizens. School personnel who do not provide sufficient and appropriate opportunities for children of poverty simply reinforce automatic failure models for these children.

This chapter examines the feminization of poverty and its unique implications for children. It also examines the origins of hopelessness as well as the interaction of the six dimensions of circular hopelessness and poverty. Research regarding the education of urban youth shows that consistent and historical poverty contributes to the creation of a sense of hopelessness that persists in a circular nature. There appear to be six interactive, systemic components of circular hopelessness that converge and negatively impinge upon the lives of urban children and their families. Consequently, the correlation of poverty and the associated circular hopelessness are discussed in this chapter. Finally, the need to establish collaboration among schools, families, communities, and social-service agencies is a critical issue. Therefore, sociocultural status, parents, urban community change, and an analysis of the psychological impact of poverty on children are examined.

THE FEMINIZATION OF POVERTY AND IMPLICATIONS FOR CHILDREN

The most significant change in poverty characteristics over the last twenty-five years has been the transition from men and women living in poverty to predominately women with children living in poor environments throughout all areas of the United States. Based on an average of 4.5 percent growth in poverty levels over the last ten years, the anticipated urban poverty population should be near 43.2 percent today. The poverty rate for children attending urban schools is often near or above seventy percent in most communities. Rodgers (1986) indicated that significantly different rates of change in poverty levels occurred among the various social, demographic, and geographic groups. In other words, poverty is perhaps the one variable that transcends race, geographic region, and other social and political issues.

Rodgers also indicated that the populations living in poverty are now less rural and more urban; the proportion of the poverty population living in central cities has increased from 31.9 percent in 1970 to 36.4 percent in 1980. Knox (1988) noted that although women have become a larger fraction of the poor, the more significant change has been that poor women in the past were likely to be the wives of poor men. Now they are more often heads of their own households. This feminization of the poor has occurred among both African-Americans and whites. However, African-American female-headed households account for the most dramatic increase in the poverty population. Needless to say, the feminization of poverty has increased the proportion of children in the poverty population. In 1985, there were more children living below the poverty line than at any time since the early 1960s (Knox, 1988). Furthermore, according to Knox, more than half of all poor children currently live in female-headed households, compared to less than twenty-five percent in the early 1960s. Wilson (1987) has argued that the intensity and complexity of issues affecting the poor, especially those concerning children, require a comprehensive and coordinated strategy involving macroeconomics policies combined with fiscal and monetary policies.

Leaders in the educational and social-service environments must ask some very challenging questions. For example, what can schools and social-service agencies do to address the growing need of children who live in poverty? Do children develop hopeless behaviors as a result of their poverty, and do schools and social-service agencies contribute to these feelings of hopelessness? Is there a cyclical relationship between poor parents and their interactions with various institutions within our culture? Do children adopt similar attitudes and beliefs regarding what they observe of their parents? The primary challenge or question focuses on what schools and social-service agencies can do to arrest this cyclical nature of hopelessness.

CHILDREN AND POVERTY

Children are the individuals most adversely affected by the hopelessness that poverty creates. They are the least able to combat or change the psychosocial elements of their environments. Adults and parents have either been unwilling or unable to transform their environment, and consequently, the psychological impact of the environment leaves a tremendous amount of responsibility on social-change agents in our culture, namely, teachers, social workers, parents, community and civic leaders, therapists, medical personnel, and others who deal directly with these at-risk populations. Unique questions for schools and social-service agencies follow: What can be done? What is our role? What can the school and social-service agencies do to ensure that all members of the organization adopt policies and principles to ensure success for children impacted by poverty?

PERSISTENT AND CURRENT POVERTY

Persistent poverty refers to more severe economic deprivation. Devine, Plunkett, and Wright (1992) suggest that chronic stress caused by economic deprivation has been linked to poor mental health. McLeod and Shanahan (1993) indicated that people subjected to persistent poverty significantly internalize symptoms above and beyond the effect of current poverty. In other words, the increased internalization causes additional stress that families living in poverty endure. Theorists who support the persistent poverty implications believe the perception of significant loss rather than the actual loss itself worsens conditions for those living in chronic poverty.

Current poverty refers to present levels of stress associated with a recent poverty status. Families in current poverty are those who are affected by immediate financial difficulties, such as major difficulty in paying bills or the threat of repossession of a vehicle or home. Researchers suggest that current poverty may be more harmful than persistent poverty because it more strongly predicts current levels of stress.

An additional factor to be considered when studying poverty and children is the manner by which race and ethnic groups experience different kinds of poverty. For example, poor African-Americans and Hispanics are more likely than poor Anglos to live in isolated urban ghettos (U.S. Bureau of the Census, 1986, p.15). African-Americans enter poverty with fewer economic resources than Anglos and are less likely to have family members with resources to loan (McLoyd, 1990). Regardless of race and ethnicity, however, American children are affected by poverty, and the psychological implications are that systemic and individual changes are necessary for consistent, productive, and successful mobility from poverty to non-poverty status. Because of persistent and current poverty dilemmas, social isolation, economic disparity, and various psychosocial influences, adults and children of poverty are faced with major psychological and emotional hurdles.

THE ORIGINS OF HOPELESSNESS

Hopelessness denotes a sense of despondency, desperation, and grief associated with a concern or particular issue. Hopelessness creates feelings of futility, abandonment of oneself to a seemingly inevitable fate, and typically suggests there is little to no intellectual judgment concerning negative probabilities. In other words, individuals who experience hopelessness essentially feel there is absolutely nothing that can be done to change their condition. The origins of current problems pertaining to the successful matriculation of underrepresented populations throughout mainstream American culture can typically be traced to issues of inequality and feelings of hopelessness.

The manner by which our culture defines, separates, and allocates resources is the primary determiner of class and structure. Poverty has always played a major role in American society, for children have always been assigned to social standing based on the affluence of their parents. While American society would never consider itself a classical caste-oriented system, there are clear examples of caste-oriented labels assigned to poor adults and especially children of poverty. Generations of underrepresented populations have endured inferior schools, substandard housing, menial jobs, and the indignities of poverty (Bell, 1991; Kelly, 1992a; Miller, 1992; Moss, 1991). Michael Harrington's *The Other America* (1962), the forerunner of the Economic Opportunity Act of 1964, focused on eliminating poverty by 1976, our nation's 200th anniversary. It is apparent, however, that urban and rural populations alike are still adversely affected by poverty and low income, thus creating and maintaining an at-risk population in need of transformation.

Since the poverty line was first developed in 1965, educators and policymakers have tried to develop policies and programs that positively impact at-risk populations. Politicians and educators alike have searched for effective strategies to address poor and at-risk populations. However, it is imperative that they first have a complete understanding of the interconnectedness of major American institutions, poverty populations, and attitudes and perceptions of hopelessness. The ability to create such programming has been made more difficult by the conceptual reality of circular hopelessness.

CIRCULAR HOPELESSNESS AND POVERTY

As indicated earlier, this chapter takes the position that underrepresented populations experience severe negative interactions with at least six major systemic institutions within American culture. Circular hopelessness suggests that these social institutions develop unwritten rules and norms regarding their interactions with poor adults. The six social institutions govern (a) the legal system, (b) the financial system, (c) politics and political parties, (d) health care and the family, (e) social services, and (f) business and career socialization. These social institutions have consistently negative interactions with poor and impoverished individuals that ultimately result in a severe feeling of hopelessness that becomes cyclical. As a result of these continuing negative interactions, poor populations surrounding urban schools develop a sense of psychological hopelessness that is transferred to children in urban schools and social-service institutions within the community. Circular hopelessness also suggests that these institutions are interconnected and serve to limit and decrease poor children's opportunities to move successfully in positive directions in school and mainstream society. When individuals from impoverished backgrounds interact with these six social institutions, they are likely to experience rejection, despondency, grief, unfairness, racism, discrimination, bias, mistreatment, and inequality. The unplanned interconnectedness of the six institutions and the negative consequences experienced by poor urban residents results in hopelessness behavior. Psychological hopelessness exists, which can lead to concerns for social desirability, depression, life stress, chronic and acute lowering of self-esteem, loneliness, dysfunctional cognitions, psychological distress, powerlessness, and family maladjustment. It is therefore logical to assume that the children of the poor who attend urban schools are children of circular hopelessness.

It is critical to point out that the six major social institutional and systemic components of circular hopelessness also play a positive role in the lives of families and especially children living in urban America. Often, interaction with these institutions and the corresponding benefits that families receive are the only avenues connecting them with some level of meaning and purpose to life. Although there is constant political debate about federal resources made available to poor Americans, these monies often do not provide an opportunity for individuals to change their social standing in life. Positive benefits notwithstanding, the circle of hopelessness continues.

Brofenhenner (1976) provides an ecological perspective of how microsystems (family and community) and macrosystems (governmental, social, educational, and economic policies) pose challenges and opportunities for poor children. Brofenhenner's perspective needs to be extended to identify specifically (a) the role of poverty in generating feelings of hopelessness, (b) the way the six major institutions in American society contribute to the development and maintenance of circular hopelessness in the lives of urban children, and (c) the impact of circular hopelessness on educational achievement.

Although the counseling and psychology fields can provide more in-depth descriptions of the psychological impact of hopelessness, it seems obvious to suggest that concerns about social desirability, depression, life stress, chronic and acute lowering of self-esteem, loneliness, dysfunctional cognitions, psychological distress, powerlessness, and family maladjustment are related to the circular hopelessness that urban children are socialized to feel.

THE SIX INSTITUTIONAL COMPONENTS OF CIRCULAR HOPELESSNESS

As a result of the high level of poverty and the degree of hopelessness experienced by urban poor populations, it becomes obvious that there are severe negative implications for urban children. These institutions are referred to as social not only because they involve people, but also because the people within these institutions often have individualized authority and decision-making power when interacting with adults from low income environments. The six social institutions will be discussed regarding their impact on the at-risk, underrepresented poor populations and children from urban schools.

LEGAL HOPELESSNESS

The legal system participates in circular hopelessness by sending the message (real or imagined) that a disproportionate number of minorities and other traditionally underrepresented populations are more negatively impacted by the legal system than other populations. It has been commonly discussed that people in poor, urban communities face the increased possibility of arrest for acts and behavior that would be ignored in suburban or rural communities. One classic example is the discretion police officers have regarding traffic violations. There is a common belief that members of poor urban communities are unlikely to receive any casual forgiveness for minor traffic violations, such as speeding or not yielding at a stop sign. Research suggests that urban community members may have some cause for concern. African-American males between the ages of twenty and twenty-nine represent twenty-three percent of those in prison, on parole, or on probation and are only six percent of the population. Also, the overall imprisonment rate for African-American males is 1,092 per 100,000 as compared to 164 per 100,000 for Anglo males (Nelson, 1991). For many African-American boys in urban schools, going to jail has become a type of "rite of passage" to adulthood. It is easy to see how the events that children observe in their community can become part of their dream as they grow up. In other words, urban children can become socialized by their environment to the extent that moral and ethical decision-making may not be consistent with the values and social orientation of the larger society.

During the last ten years, two court cases captured unprecedented national interest and the imagination of the American public. The Rodney King trial and the O. J. Simpson trial crystallized two significant and contrasting views regarding the urban poor and their attitudes regarding the hopelessness experience within the legal system. The purpose of this chapter or book is not to determine guilt or innocence in these cases, but rather to analyze (a) feelings of hopelessness of traditionally underrepresented individuals living in poverty, (b) the implication of those feelings for school leaders, and (c) the connection of these events and feelings to circular hopelessness.

The Rodney King incident, which involved a videotape of police beating Mr. King and the subsequent not-guilty verdicts for the police involved in the beating, can be perceived to validate a belief among most minority circles: the legal system is institutionally biased against them. The underprivileged experience a feeling of hopelessness and reflect attitudes that there is essentially little or nothing that can be done to change the legal system. It was commonly heard in African-American communities during the Rodney King trial that the beating was nothing new and that it happened often in communities throughout the country. The difference in the Rodney King incident was that the entire interaction was displayed on tape and thus, made denying the event difficult. Why was there the kind of reaction in the Los Angeles community following the not-guilty verdicts in the Rodney King trial? Why did people, who are already impoverished, burn and destroy businesses in their own communities? Time and content-related information does not allow me to expand into these specific perspectives. However, it can be argued that the individuals in those communities were hopeless and perceived that no recourse was available other than to respond in that manner. Cornel West, author of *Race Matters* (1992), suggested that the Los Angeles riots, which erupted following the Rodney King verdict, were not actually riots but a response by a generation who felt hopelessness and despair.

What were the symbolic lessons that urban school children learned from the Rodney King incident? Many would argue that school children learned that even when a person is caught beating an African-American man on videotape, the legal system will not support your efforts if you are from an underrepresented population. There is sufficient perception in the urban community that there is no justice for people of color in the criminal justice system; justice, they have learned, is for anyone except them.

The O. J. Simpson saga is extremely complicated. However, there are at least three significant social messages that young, urban African-American males likely received from the first O. J. Simpson trial: (a) the importance of race, (b) the validation of a common belief in the African-American community that the legal system will conspire against African-American males or "set them up" in order to find guilt, and (c) the perception of the power of money. While there is significant debate about O. J. Simpson's guilt or innocence and his genuiness to the African-American community, there was little doubt among African-Americans regarding the role that race played in this case. All of the polls and surveys clearly indicated that African-Americans and whites were essentially split on Mr. Simpson's guilt or innocence. African-Americans did not understand why their white colleagues or neighbors could not understand that the police department conspired against him and whites could not understand why African-Americans could not see the obvious guilt in this case.

The second significant social message that African-American males in urban schools received from this example of legal hopelessness is the belief that if O. J. Simpson can be "set up," then they could also be "set up." While conspiracy theories are typically discounted in mainstream America, especially when it comes to police corruption, these theories are alive and well in the African-American community. African-American boys grow up believing that police are not trustworthy and once they are involved in the "system," there is little hope for escape.

Some contended the O. J. Simpson case was more reflective of power and money or at least the perception of such. Most individuals living in urban communities would indicate that the reason Mr. Simpson is a free man today is because of his power and money. Urban youth may believe that if Mr. Simpson did not have fame and fortune that he would likely be in jail today. Although there is sufficient research to suggest that the chances of making it in professional athletics is limited, many urban students are brokering their lives on being the next American sports superstar.

FINANCIAL HOPELESSNESS

Financial institutions, which are the lifeblood of any organized and industrialized society, also contribute to circular hopelessness. Underrepresented populations, by virtue of their home address, are considered known entities to lending institutions and decisions are often made on the basis of their race and socioeconomic status. Financial institutions have been accused and convicted of discriminatory loan practices so often that these stories are no longer considered newsworthy.

Recently, a nationally televised news program documented the experiences of two male college graduates (one African-American and the other Anglo) with identical college degrees and professional credentials as they moved to a Midwestern town and began to secure an apartment, a job, and to purchase an automobile. In each instance the African-American had more difficulty securing an apartment and was often told that the apartment was rented when just moments earlier the apartment had been available. A higher price was quoted to the African-American than to the Anglo-American for the same automobile. While one could easily argue that this incident was a one-time occurrence, the national news program conducted the same experiment in a different city with the same adult males and the results were validated.

Although underrepresented populations have the same credit histories as their Anglo-American counterparts, it is well documented that minority applicants are more likely to be rejected by loan committees and financial boards for loans and credit lines (except for cars and other disposable items that will increase debt but not the accumulation of wealth). The inability of underrepresented populations to secure positive relationships with financial institutions adversely affects their standard of living, purchasing power, home ownership, and overall social and financial self-esteem. Consequently, the children of underrepresented populations perceive that this interaction between their population and institutional structures within our culture is standard, acceptable, and the norm. When underrepresented populations, and especially urban students, continue to receive these negative messages from financial institutions, they begin to accept this interaction as a way of life and conduct their lives under the umbrella of circular hopelessness.

POLITICAL HOPELESSNESS

Political affiliation and power are important for all members of a culture. Political affiliation and influence allow individuals or groups to feel empowered with some control over the immediate environment. The political vote and support of underrepresented populations have often been courted by politicians from both the Democratic and Republican parties. Underrepresented groups are again connected to the theory of circular hopelessness in the sense that although they are often courted during election years, their overall economic and social conditions typically remain the same. Hence, the phrase, "the rich get richer and the poor stay poor" has validity in the lives of urban poor people. Politicians in urban and rural areas frequently attend church services and picnics organized by underrepresented groups as a means of obtaining their endorsement. All too often the vote is sought, but rarely is there follow-through by the politicians. As a result, this interaction leads to low expectations and cynicism toward the political system.

During the past several presidential elections, a major question that has been asked in the African-American community is "Should the black community as a whole continue to support Democratic candidates?" More precisely, "Has the Democratic party taken the African-American vote for granted?" If there is movement in terms of collective support for another political party, should that party be the Republican party or should the African-American vote become independent? Often in underrepresented communities there is the feeling that they must select the lesser of two evils.

Clearly, some underrepresented individuals from poverty backgrounds have succeeded in the current system by ascending to middle- and upper-middle-class status and many have achieved high socioeconomic status. However, the overwhelming majority of underrepresented groups are confined to the urban inner-city and are largely uneducated, in despair, and hopeless. Social and political theorists have strongly suggested that the Reagan-Bush era did not serve children of poverty well and contend that military spending increased at the expense of social programs, specifically programs that involved food, shelter, and educational training for underrepresented populations.

HEALTH AND FAMILY ISSUES

Health and family concerns for children of poverty are of great importance for social workers, teachers, and medical personnel. Children of poverty are unlikely to receive appropriate prenatal care, are subject to more illnesses, and are less likely to receive routine medical attention. They often receive medical care only in the cases of emergency. McLeod and Shanahan (1993) reported that poor children experience greater psychological distress than do more affluent children. They reported that the relationship among poverty, parenting behaviors, and children's mental health do not vary by race and ethnicity and called for greater emphasis on family processes in studies of children's poverty. Once again, race and ethnicity are not significant when there is evidence of consistent poverty. Regarding the family, McLoyd (1990) suggested a major link exists between economic hardship and parenting behavior. She further posits that subsequent psychological distress is derived from an excess of negative life events and chronic undesirable conditions. Liem and Liem (1978) noted "individuals who are poor are confronted with an unremitting succession of negative life events in the context of chronically stressful, ongoing life conditions such as inadequate housing and dangerous neighborhoods that together increase the exigencies of day to day existence" (p. 140). The consequences of stress associated with poverty are well documented. Therefore, children are impacted in such a way that connects the circular hopelessness theory with health and family issues.

SOCIAL SERVICES HOPELESSNESS

Social services offer critical support for many less fortunate individuals in our society. However, for underrepresented populations the stigma associated with social services contributes to their degree of despair and hopelessness. The literature documents the impact of the economic hardship and psychological distress associated with poverty. Social services were initially created as a means of helping people through temporary difficult times, but have led to a bureaucratic system that defines people on the basis of status and class. Perhaps the most significant variable regarding social services and circular hopelessness is the notion that one feels inferior, embarrassed, and hopeless. In addition to those feelings are major societal concerns such as racism, gender discrimination, class and caste restrictions. The children of poverty are placed once again in a seemingly hopeless situation.

BUSINESS AND CAREER SOCIALIZATION

Based on the previous five variables, it is logical to assert that the interconnectedness of circular hopelessness has a direct impact on business and career options available to poverty-stricken populations. Underrepresented populations who have experienced negative interactions with the legal, financial, political, health, and social-services institutions would be less likely than other groups to have positive interactions with employment prospects. Initially, there is a strong possibility that individuals from traditionally underrepresented communities and impoverished environments will lack a sufficient level of education to meet minimal job requirements. Because of the need for education, these individuals are typically relegated to service-oriented jobs which normally pay minimum wage. These low wages cause additional conflict due to limited purchasing power, the high cost of day-care facilities, and the esteem associated with jobs that have little opportunity for advancement.

Another example of hopelessness in business and career options is the presence of a "glass ceiling." Glass ceilings are perceived to be invisible, institutionally-imposed limits or barriers placed on women and underrepresented populations of men. The glass ceiling ensures that a woman (or underrepresented individual) will only be able to be promoted to certain levels within an organization and that chief executive offices are retained for males only. Women continually discuss limitations placed on them in a predominately male-oriented business and industrial world. If women who are educated, articulate, and willing to work extremely hard for promotions perceive limits, one can only imagine the despair experienced by underrepresented populations from poor environments.

Again, following yet another negative interaction with social institutions, poor populations are left in a hopeless condition. Often poor families are caught between low-skilled, minimum-wage employment and the need for government subsidized health benefits. Mothers with children will likely opt for appropriate care for their children before they commit to a minimum-wage job with no medical benefits.

COMBATING CIRCULAR HOPELESSNESS

There appear to be only two ways that underrepresented poor populations can reverse the circular hopelessness that impedes the achievement of a positive standard of living. The first measure is through some form of spiritual transformation, such a religious experience or some form of communication with a higher power. Although many might quickly dismiss this approach as having no merit, it deserves consideration. For example, the black church has historically played a critical and influential role in the African-American community. The church has not only served as a spiritual meeting place, but it has also served as a community standard bearer for social, political, and familial interaction. There is considerable debate about the current effectiveness of the African-American church. The church remains as one of the only institutions within the African-American community that has a stable financial, social, and political base. It is no secret that most of the civil-rights leaders established their foundations in the church. The African-American church has long been the training ground for most leaders in the urban community and it seems logical that the church could still play a role in urban reform and serve as an instrument to combat circular hopelessness. This type of intervention requires that individuals be able to understand the way circular hopelessness operates and implement a spiritual plan so the circular hopelessness cycle does not continue to impact them the same way. African-American churches could develop and offer such programs to members of their congregations.

The second measure to reverse circular hopelessness requires intellectual transformation. An intellectual transformation occurs when an individual experiences a cognitive, behavioral, and affective change in his or her values and beliefs. As a result of this change, there is direct action which is related to the decision-making process. In other words, it becomes clear to individuals that there is an unspoken, institutionalized process that is primarily aimed at thwarting underrepresented individuals in low socioeconomic environments.

A step that schools and social-service agencies can initiate and sustain incorporates proactive behavior. This behavior demands an understanding of circular hopelessness and the impact of the interconnectedness of the theory that has essentially crippled an entire generation of underrepresented people.

Given the grim reality of children in poverty and the likelihood of immeasurable emotional and psychological damage to these young people, it becomes paramount that those working in poverty-stricken, urban environments establish positive and creative strategies to reverse the negative consequences of circular hopelessness. Also, given the widespread implications of circular hopelessness and the impact on children, it is important to develop strategies and approaches to address circular hopelessness, the needs of children, and poverty in general. The following approaches are offered:

- *Clearly explain to children that their socioeconomic status is not a result of their own doing (or perhaps that of their parents), but rather a consequence of social and economic situations.* Parents and those working with children must convey techniques (e.g., completing school work, abiding by the law, following directions, communicating appropriately, and seeking appropriate role models) and strategies (e.g., maintaining good school attendance and grades, following directions of parents and role models, resisting negative peer pressure, and becoming involved with after-school and summer activities that promote positive self-esteem and strong self-identity of children of poverty) help the children identify their role in relationship to the rest of the society.

- *Set quality standards of conduct and behavior.* These quality standards are very important and must be initiated by parents and policymakers and then communicated to children. It is critical that children not only listen to what we say but also observe what we do. It is critical that adults model appropriate behaviors for children to observe and adopt. In essence, the quality standards become significant measuring items as adults observe children and as children observe adults.

♦ *Create a positive and accepting psychological environment for success at school and home.* Parents, school administrators, and social workers must create the vision in the mind of children that, although their tangible environment is depressing (and in despair), it does not mean that they have to conduct themselves in a way that mirrors the environment. These comments must be combined with supportive techniques (such as rewards for grades and behavior, and field trips to museums, art galleries, libraries, and institutions of higher learning).

♦ *Communicate with children on an intellectual basis about difficult and controversial issues such as sex, drugs, and standards of behavior.* An appropriate amount of time should be allotted for reflection and processing. Parents must establish a communication pattern that allows their views to be directly transmitted and not allow other media, such as movies, magazines, and music videos, to dictate their childrens' decisions regarding social issues.

♦ *Discuss race in a contextual framework with children of poverty.* Children in poverty-stricken environments learn at an early age the significance of race. They also learn quickly that a disproportionate number of underrepresented populations are affected by poverty and circular hopelessness. A discussion in the family and school about race from a historical, social, political, and economic context is necessary for children of poverty to connect cognitively with realistic issues that confront them on a daily basis. It seems logical to suggest that when one possesses the cognitive ability to analyze and synthesize an event or situation, it allows that individual to make more rational decisions regarding behavior and responses.

ADDITIONAL SIGNIFICANT FACTORS FOR URBAN COMMUNITIES

There are several additional factors that impact children from urban schools who live in impoverished environments: (a) sociocultural issues regarding school achievement and children of poverty, (b) the role of parents and urban community change, and (c) children and the violence in their lives.

SOCIOCULTURAL STATUS: SCHOOL ACHIEVEMENT AND CHILDREN OF POVERTY

Numerous studies have indicated a correlation between sociocultural status and performance on achievement tests (Hale and Benson, 1989; Jensen, 1969; Myers, 1991; Obgu, 1985; Williams and Leonard, 1989). Ornstein and Levine (1990) have attempted to explain this relationship by noting the distinctions between parental and school rules which make it difficult for lower socioeconomic students to follow school procedures when there are apparent differences in communication styles, and terminology between the student and the school. Because of lowered academic standards for children of poverty, there is negative peer pressure upon students from lower sociocultural backgrounds and "as terminology and concepts become increasingly abstract, many lower class (and students from working-class homes) fall further behind" (p.13). There is additional peer pressure felt by urban school students who are making every attempt to complete assigned tasks and school assignments and who desperately want to succeed. The peer pressure comes from classmates who criticize the students for "acting white" or for trying to be the teacher's pet. The "acting white" criticism is particularly difficult at the elementary level, because few students are mature enough to choose to be ostracized by their peers. Students have reported hiding their grade cards from their peers so their high grades would not be seen or changing an A grade to F before their friends could see the actual grade.

Students from low-income homes may be considered to be slow learners and are frequently set apart with instruction given at a slower pace, thus contributing to a wider gap in achievement. Moreover, differences in teacher and student backgrounds and dialects make it difficult for middle-class teachers to understand and motivate children from backgrounds in poverty . Middle-class teachers tend to reject lower-class students' lifestyles and culture.

> . . . [B]ecause students are influenced by their teachers' perceptions and behaviors, low teacher expectations generate further declines in students' motivation and performance. By the time low achieving students reach upper elementary grades or junior high school, they are required to accomplish very little and low performance becomes acceptable to their teachers. Frequently, teachers give up trying to teach low achievers or seek less frustrating work (Levine, 1990, p.11-12).

Numerous studies have shown that student performance often parallels teacher expectations (Dent, 1989; Hale, 1982; Neisser, 1985; Pollard, 1989) and that children achieve at higher levels in classrooms where teachers nurture and encourage them (Ford, 1985; Jones, 1986; Smith and Chunn, 1989; and Waxman, 1989). Thus a major contributor to the lack of academic success for many children of poverty may be low teacher expectations (Dent, 1989; Irvine, 1990).

Low teacher expectations have also been shown to lead to placement in special education classes (Irvine, 1990). For example, African-American children are more than twice as likely as white children to be placed in special education classes, but less likely than white children to be placed in gifted and talented classes (Ogbu, 1974, 1985). Also, Irvine (1990) concluded that many teachers judge a student's ability to perform in school by superficial characteristics. She further noted that teachers ". . . sometimes make judgments based on the way a child is dressed in class or on what they can surmise about a child's family. Because of racism in our culture, they often make the judgment based on skin color" (p. 55).

THE ROLE OF PARENTS AND URBAN COMMUNITY CHANGE

There is common agreement among social scientists, sociologists, researchers, professors, politicians, preachers, and reformers in all social, economic, and political arenas that parents may be the most important factor in (a) promoting student achievement in school, (b) guiding children through difficult peer decision-making processes, (c) assisting in selection techniques regarding friends, marriage partners, job interest, and (d) helping with the comprehensive interactions and procedures that occur from birth to adulthood. While parents play a critical role in the success of their children, we can not underestimate the influence of poverty on the psychological and emotional status of children.

McLoyd (1990) provides a depressing description of parents and children living in urban areas by suggesting that of the approximately 9.7 million African-American children, nearly half are classified as poor and face an inevitable number of social and economic battles that most middle-class persons do not understand. Also, to highlight the implications of poverty and its impact on one underrepresented population, the National Black Child Development Institute (NBCDI) noted that between 1973 and 1986, the poverty rate of young African-American families with parents under twenty-five rose from below forty-four to sixty-two percent. In addition, according to NBCDI, among single-parent, African-American families (usually female headed) two-thirds of the children live in poverty.

A study by Hashima and Amato (1994) revealed that parents living in poverty may have a greater need for social support than affluent, upper middle-class parents and parents of higher socioeconomic status. The study also indicated that poor parents experience more chronic stress, due to difficulty in paying bills, living in substandard housing, poor quality medical care, and the risk of victimization. A final comparison of poor parents to more affluent parents suggested that affluent parents can purchase services (e.g., child-care) to reduce parental strain and ease their parental demands.

The literature documents economic hardship and related influences on parental interaction with children who live in poverty. Many studies have revealed that as a family's economic situation worsens, parents are less nurturing and discipline their children more inconsistently (Lempers, Clark-Lempers, and Simmons, 1989; McLoyd and Wilson, 1991). Additional research

has revealed that incidences of maltreatment are disproportionately large among families in poverty (Gelles, 1989; U.S. Advisory Board on Child Abuse and Neglect, 1990). For example, a
1989 study by Gelles found an inverse relationship between
parental income and parental violence. Parents with incomes
below the poverty line had the highest rates of violence toward
children (twenty-two percent), while families with incomes ex-
ceeding $20,000 had the lowest rates of violence (eleven per-
cent). Also, a research report by Wolock and Horowitz in 1979
noted that even among welfare recipients, those who had engaged in maltreatment, compared with those who did not, had
more children, lived under poorer material circumstances, had
more socioeconomic challenges and deprivation in childhood,
and were more socially isolated. As a final example, Gelles (1989)
suggested that economic deprivation is the reason why single
mothers, who make up nearly ninety percent of all single parents, are more likely than married mothers to abuse their children physically.

Needless to say, financial difficulties can fuel family conflict
and criticism. Much of this conflict and criticism is aimed toward those in the family with the least ability to provide or de-
fend themselves. For example, in a study by Strauss, Gelles,
and Steinmetz (1980), the rate of child abuse among fathers
employed part-time was almost twice as high as the rate among
fathers employed full-time.

Caution should be exercised, however, with regard to the
interpretation of these findings. One criticism often voiced in
the urban community is that the reason that reports of the incidents regarding family instability are much higher than in other
communities is because there are sufficient workers in the urban community to record the interaction. In other words, there
is a common belief that there are as many difficulties in other
communities, but these incidents are not reported as often. Readers should note that these studies are not exhaustive: every urban family does not experience, behave, or respond in a fashion
consistent with the findings of any study. Each urban family
should be treated as unique and not as a number.

With more Americans descending into poverty (especially
underrepresented populations), more attention should be fo-

cused on the psychological well-being of children as well as strategies for promoting optimal parental behavior. Cohen and Wills (1985) indicated that there has been a renewed interest in offering social support in the prevention and treatment of child abuse. Focusing on the environment of families and on manifestations of family stress, "the likelihood of child maltreatment varies in direct relation to the availability, adequacy, and use made of a family's supportive resources in the community" (Garbarino and Crouter, 1978, p. 604).

Perhaps the most elusive factors are the unknown impact poverty has on children and what parents and schools can do to decrease the role poverty plays in the lives of these young people. Children, once again, are the individuals impacted by the parents' relationship and interactions within circular hopelessness.

Reginald Clark (1983) supports the position that there is no one way to raise a child but rather proposes that the essence of positive family life is found in the culture of the family. Essentially, any significant outcomes and successes that children exhibit are results of the values, beliefs, traditions, mores, and policies established and enforced by members of the household. Without question, any significant change in urban communities must involve the input, advice, counsel, and recommendations of urban families.

SUMMARY

Circular hopelessness is primarily concerned with underrepresented populations and contends that these populations experience negative interactions with all major social institutions. Because of this negative interaction, a cyclical or circular interconnectedness exists that serves to provide little or no hope for escaping the hopelessness. Circular hopelessness contends that children whose parents are victims of circular hopelessness will essentially acquire the psychological chains of hopelessness and thereby create another generation of urban dwellers who see "no way out" of their situations.

In this chapter we examined a theory that discusses the social, economic, and political phenomena that affect underrepresented populations and the interaction of those underrepresented populations with six systemic, social institutions. Circular hopelessness suggests that as underrepresented populations exchange and interact with these institutional areas (legal, financial, political, health and family, social services, and business and career socialization), there are continuous negative consequences.

Sociologists have argued for some time that the answer to poverty is extremely complex and involves such solutions as job creation, retraining programs, welfare reform, educational reform, housing investment, in addition to a certain amount of spatial, racial, and client-specific targeting. Given the nature of circular hopelessness, policymakers must begin to investigate integrative and collaborative efforts to address poverty. Schools must also begin to initiate programs that combine with social and economic agencies to address children of poverty who are also children of circular hopelessness. Social-service agencies must utilize school organizations as a means of demonstrating the importance of education to poverty-stricken families. While additional research is valuable and necessary to test the validity of the circular hopelessness theory, one cannot ignore that it appears the interactions of poverty and continuous negative consequences with systemic social institutions cause obvious difficulties in our culture. The obvious question is which combination of programs or policies is most appropriate to a particular group, especially in light of circular hopelessness?

When one encounters a person who has lost hope, intellectual transformation is a key step toward change. This cognitive step requires that schools and social-service agencies combine efforts to eliminate the stigma associated with children of poverty. While most professionals have had some form of sensitivity training, one can not overstate the importance of children's self-esteem, positive attitude, and understanding the role perceptions play in our interaction with children. Professionals should remember that children are often very astute and quickly recognize negative feelings based on appearance (e.g., style of clothing).

While compiling documentation for this book, I had the opportunity to talk to a retired senior citizen who can be classified as an underrepresented population member born into a caste-oriented, poor environment. This woman with eleven children described her meager surroundings and shared the story of how her own mother had used folded paper bags for shoes and how clothing was washed every evening in order to have clean clothing for the next day. Perhaps the most significant perspective that emerged from this interview was that this mother was able to encourage the development of high self-esteem and personal motivation. She explained their socioeconomic status to her children, saying "this was not the way life was supposed to be." In essence, there are family-oriented values and responsibilities that poor adults must develop, maintain, and share with all family members. It is apparent that intellectual transformation must take place in order to create an opportunity for children of poverty to challenge their circumstances.

Before any substantial and long-lasting change can take place children must be able to cognitively understand who they are and how their status came to be. However, the systemic institutional variables in our society cannot go unchanged. School officials, social-service workers, and policymakers in all arenas must address the process, manner, and procedure they employ to interact with adults and children of poverty. Institutions need to focus on their internal authority so that those most adversely affected by their policies and procedures will have the opportunity for equality and justice. Institutions must take the initiative to eliminate bias and discrimination in their programs, policies, and organizations. Circular hopelessness has become ingrained in our consciousness and is, unfortunately, a real element in our institutional power and decision-making structure. Elimination of this debilitating, systemic circular hopelessness can be accomplished through a collaborative effort between underrepresented populations and majority populations that include honest communication and creative problem-solving.

The traditional recommendations to bring about substantial change include those suggested by the Eisenhower Foundation:

- ♦ Early intervention and urban school reform
- ♦ Establishment of a youth-investment corporation

- ◆ Reforming existing school-to-work transition programs
- ◆ A community-enterprise development strategy for the inner city
- ◆ Increased funding for drug abuse prevention and treatment
- ◆ Community–based coalitions to prevent violence
- ◆ Black male classrooms or schools
- ◆ Mentoring and manhood-development programs
- ◆ Multicomponent community centers
- ◆ Community policing

It is clear that any strategic plan or approach must include all levels of community involvement. When we, as a society, finally agree that these issues are important enough, then multicontextual change can be implemented.

What message do urban children receive from circular hopelessness? Essentially, urban children perceive that voting does not matter because whomever is elected will not impact their lives. Political affiliation does not carry the traditional American value of contribution and making a difference. Children in America's urban schools must be able to attach a significant and real meaning to political involvement. This requires significant stakeholders within the community to collaborate with school officials to validate and confirm meaning to political affiliation.

Given the incorrectly assumed relationship between sociocultural conditions and school achievement, school districts must address these differences, if they wish to maximize educational opportunities for all students. Also, given the far-reaching implications of circular hopelessness and its interconnectedness to other institutions within our culture, a considerable amount of attention must be directed toward the role of teachers, social-service agencies, and school administrators when there is interaction between these educational stakeholders and children of poverty.

2

ACADEMIC ACHIEVEMENT AND PARENTAL INVOLVEMENT IN URBAN SCHOOLS

The key to school improvement lies in changing the mind-set and the heart set of all members of the school community
—Ronald Edmonds

Educators generally agree that academic achievement is the singular issue or variable that can make a significant difference in the lives of individuals. The need for academic achievement is particularly significant for underrepresented populations. This chapter reviews academic achievement and examines sociocultural factors that impact academic achievement, socioeconomic status and parental involvement.

GENETIC VS. ENVIRONMENTAL EXPLANATIONS OF LOW ACHIEVEMENT

A great deal of the research conducted on the genetic disposition and achievement of minorities typically reflects relationships between African-Americans and members of the dominant culture. Much of the research relating to the academic achievement of African-Americans has involved cross-race comparative studies, which have been characterized by Pollard (1989) as a "search for the explanation of the minority student's failure" (p. 298). From these studies, two general theories have emerged as explanations for the low academic achievement of African-American students in comparison to white students: namely, a genetic theory and an environmental theory (Ornstein and Levine, 1990; Pollard, 1989).

The genetic theory has been reflected in the research of Arthur Jensen who concluded that approximately eighty percent of the variance in Intelligence Quotient (IQ) between African-Americans and white students is due to genetic differences and only twenty percent is due to causes from the environment. Jensen framed his argument as follows:

> A hypothesis that I believe comprehends more of the facts and is consistent with more of the converging lines of evidence than any other I know of, in its simplest terms, is the hypothesis that is the same within the white and black populations as between the populations, and (b) the genetic variance involved in IQ is about one-fifth less in black than the white population" (p. 10 of testimony before the U.S Senate Select Committee on Equal Educational Opportunity; Jensen, 1969, p. 20).

Jensen drew a further distinction between African-American and white populations by proposing the existence of two levels of intelligence. According to Jensen (1969) level one intelligence involves being able to think in concrete rather than abstract terms. Level two intelligence involves being able to think in abstract terms, conceptualize and solve problems. Jensen (1969) argued that level one intelligence is distributed in the lower-class, the middle-, and the upper-class alike. Level two intelligence, Jensen reports, is found mainly in the middle- and upper-classes. Jensen further contended that level-two children do well in school because "the traditional methods of classroom instruction emphasize cognitive and conceptual skills" (p. 14). Jensen also suggested that level-one children perform less well in school because the classroom methods of instruction do not utilize their inherited abilities and skills.

In contrast to this genetic explanation for low achievement, T. R. Williams summarized the environmentalist explanation as follows:

> There are critical periods, or stages, in the development of animals, including man, during which the individual is most receptive to learning from particular kinds of experiences. These periods are very limited in duration. If an experience is to become a regular part of an individual's later behavior, it has to be acquired during the critical period when the individual is most ready for that kind of experience. Earlier or later exposure to such experience will produce little or no effect on the individual's later action (Williams, 1972, p. 116).

Disproportionately lower IQ scores for African-Americans are thus better explained by children not receiving adequate stimulation from parents during the early years of development than by genetic differences. Ogbu (1974, 1985) also argued that special programs designed to assist African-American parents in providing adequate stimulation have been unsuccessful in increasing the IQ of African-Americans not because the genetic theory is correct, but because the environmentalist view has been ethnocentric in nature. Ogbu stated:

> The lower test scores of black children on intelligence tests, especially with respect to level 2 intelligence, appear to be due partly to three related factors: (1) the caste like system's long denial of blacks of adequate access to desirable jobs and other societal positions and activities that require and promote white middle class type of cognitive skills; (2) black disillusionment because of the job ceiling and related factors, which has not encouraged them to develop a cultural norm of maximizing their test scores; and (3) the symbolic meaning of intelligence tests, which may have a negative influence of black's approach to these tests (Ogbu, 1978, p. 2).

Notably, however, despite opposing views as to whether genetic or environmental factors are the "root causes" of African-Americans having disproportionately lower achievement than whites, researchers in both camps have acknowledged that sociocultural factors bear a strong relationship to school achievement. And, in comparison to whites, African-Americans are more likely to be lower in sociocultural status (Irvine, 1990 (b); Hare and Castenell, 1985; Fenn and Iwanicki, 1986).

A DISCUSSION ON I.Q.

Asa Hilliard (1990) provided an excellent analysis of the value and worth of achievement tests with a particular emphasis on IQ testing. Hilliard contends that four basic criteria should be in place in order to evaluate effectively academic achievement tests. He suggests that tests should (a) be content valid, (b) be universally appropriate for use with different groups, (c) include representative samples of the course content and should be given to a representative sample of the population under study, and (d) consider student's relative access to knowledge. A brief summary of Hilliard's point is warranted.

While reviewing academic achievement of African-Americans and African-American males in particular, there is a strong need to assure that the curriculum matches the content being assessed on the achievement test. This concept is true for all underrepresented urban student populations. Hilliard makes a compelling argument by suggesting that tests are generally a reflection of the curriculum and content that a student learns in a localized school environment. When a student takes a national standardized test, there is clear evidence that the student "will be looking at a test where nearly half the material is being seen for the first time" (p. 37). Hilliard concludes, "[it] seems irrational then to use nationally standardized tests as if the meaning of the scores in relationship to the curriculum of one school district is the same as it is for other school districts" (p. 137).

Hilliard's second point highlights the power of those individuals who make standardized tests and the arbitrary process used in determining standardized content. The opportunity to include biased content is easy and as a result there is potential of a tremendous impact on the final scores. Appropriateness of content and the philosophical experiences of test makers and takers can influence results.

Hilliard notes in his third point:

> Good academic achievement tests are said to have a representative sample of content and the test takers are said to be representative of the population that is supposed to have been exposed to the content. In the past, African-American children were not included in standardization samples. As a result, the experience of European-American children was given greater weight on the test than those of African-American children. Most recently, attempts have been made to correct this deficiency by adding more African-American students to standardization samples for nationally standardized academic achievement tests (p. 138).

Hilliard's fourth point is perhaps the variable most hotly debated in urban schools throughout the country. This issue centers on the perception that all students indeed are exposed to identical levels of knowledge and content. In other words, standardized tests make the assumption that all of the test takers have similar experiences in schools and have been exposed to similar teachers who all emphasized the same content. Hilliard notes, "observers of schools can see that few African-American students are exposed to high quality instruction (cited in Lomotey, 1989). The interpretation that is placed on their low performance tends to penalize the student rather than to direct attention toward the systems that have withheld their benefits from the African-American student" (p. 138).

Hilliard contends the same principles that apply to academic achievement tests should be applied to IQ tests. While the primary purpose of IQ has been to predict or forecast achievement, there is serious doubt whether IQ tests are indeed valid for African-Americans. Hilliard believes "the practice of using IQ tests in schools is inappropriate for the simple reason that it makes no meaningful contribution to the education of children" (p. 139). He also notes that, "[g]iven the low performance of African-American students with respect to normative performance on

IQ tests, we must ask what benefit to the children is provided through the use of such tests" (pp. 139-140).

Hilliard offers some recommendations for improving the overall testing practice, namely to continue the national dialogue about the use and implications of standardized tests. Caution should be exercised by simply adding an individual from a traditionally underrepresented group as a reviewer or writer. Hilliard noted "[m]erely being a member of a cultural group does not place a person in the position to be helpful" (p. 141).

Consequently, when looking at academic achievement of underrepresented, urban student populations—males in particular—caution should be exercised in interpreting the meaning of standardized score means. While there is a debate about the causes of low test scores for African-Americans, one can not overlook the powerful argument presented by Hilliard. Because we Americans love to be number one and distinguish ourselves from those around us, it is likely that we will always have some form of standardized testing. The major consideration is that we do not allow the test to impact the way we interact with children. The interaction between teachers and students based on the perception of a score on a standardized test is one of the challenges facing African-American students in the next century.

SOCIOECONOMIC STATUS AND ACHIEVEMENT

There continues to be a consistent debate regarding the role and importance of socioeconomic status and its relationship to academic achievement. Again, because of the significant amount of research available regarding African-American students, the focus group for this discussion will be African-American.

The low socioeconomic status of a disproportionate number of African-Americans has been documented by Dr. Dorothy Hight, president of the National Council of Negro Women, in a speech before the Committee on Banking, Housing and Urban Affairs of the United States Senate (1991). Dr. Hight noted that: "Although African-American male unemployment was still nearly twice as high as white male unemployment in the sixties, African-American male unemployment hovered around

8 percent" (p. 37). However, in the 70s and early 80s, African-American male unemployment rates were consistently near double digit numbers. For example, in 1981, the unemployment rate for African-Americans was between 14 percent and 15.9 percent and in 1983 it was an astonishing 21 percent (Hight, 1991). Subsequently, during this period, the African-American population observed an accelerated increase in female-headed households (Gibbs, 1988; Irvine, 1990a). Dr. Hight stated that: "In 1989, 11.8% of African-American married families were poor, and 46.5% of African-American female-headed households were poor, the figure for whites were 5% and 25.4%, respectively" (Committee on Banking, Housing and Urban Affairs, 1991).

Numerous studies have indicated a positive correlation between socioeconomic status and performance on achievement tests (Hess, 1995; Jensen, 1969; Gilmore, 1985; Myers, 1991; Ogbu, 1985; Walker and Madhere, 1987; Williams and Leonard, 1989). The state of Ohio has recently adopted proficiency exams at various grade levels in elementary, middle, and high schools. Some of the preliminary findings suggest a strong correlation between wealth districts and non-wealthy school districts. The case for distinction regarding socioeconomic status and achievement can also be made with respect to students within the same school systems. Students with higher socioeconomic status tend to be assigned to higher-level classes, are involved in more school activities, and typically score higher on achievement tests.

Moreover, differences in teacher and student backgrounds and dialects make it difficult for middle class teachers to understand and motivate lower-class students. Middle-class teachers tend to reject lower-class students' lifestyles and culture, and "because students are influenced by their teachers' perceptions and behaviors, low teacher expectation generate further declines in students' motivation and performance. By the time low achieving students reach upper elementary grades or junior high school, they are required to accomplish very little and low performance becomes acceptable to their teachers. Frequently, teachers give up trying to teach low achievers or seek less frustrating work" (pp. 11–12).

A major contributor to the lack of academic success for many African-Americans may thus be low teacher expectations (Dent,

1989; Irvine, 1990b). Numerous studies have shown that student performance often parallels teacher expectations (Dent, 1989; Hale, 1982; Jackson, 1988; Neisser, 1986; Pollard, 1989) and that children achieve at higher levels in classrooms where teachers nurture and encourage them (Ford, 1985; Jones, 1986; Sowell, 1976; Smith and Chun, 1989 and Waxman, 1989). Low teacher expectations also have been shown to lead to placement in special education classes (Irvine, 1990). African-American children are more than twice as likely as white children to be placed in special education classes, but less than half as likely as white children to be placed in classes for gifted and talented children (Ogbu, 1974; 1985). Many teachers judge a student's abilities to perform in school by superficial characteristics. As noted in chapter one, "teachers, who are products of a racist culture, judge children and their prospects for academic achievement based on their ill-informed assumptions about a child's dress and the child's family and based on the child's skin color" (Irvine, 1990, p. 55).

Another interesting perspective regarding teachers involves the current argument about the need for African-American teachers being used only for African-American students. Abigail Thernstrom (1991) provided an interesting argument when she suggested that what African-American students need is good teachers, specifically those who have superior verbal skills. Thernstrom noted "teachers expected to educate kids must themselves be well educated" (p. 24). In conjunction with the role of teachers and urban male students, Johnson, Brookover, and Farrell (1991) found that if teachers fail to encourage urban students and to push them to attain substantial academic achievement subsequent failure often results in feelings of futility and low achievement. The authors noted that the failure of teachers to press some students for high achievement reinforces students' perceptions that teachers do not care whether they (a) get bad grades, (b) receive marginal grades, as long as they pass, and (c) do not exhibit strong academic work behaviors.

Strickland (1994) provided five valuable recommendations to enhance and positively impact academic achievement for urban African-American students:

- Foster a sense of community and interconnectedness within each classroom and throughout each school. Keep class size small and students in manageable groups. Create an atmosphere where each student receives individual recognition within a larger context of self as well as establish a bond between the student and teacher, which typically leads to an enhanced relationship.

- Avoid long-term ability grouping and tracking. While there is considerable debate about grouping students by ability and achievement, it would appear that Strickland's suggestion—that school leaders merge ability grouping and incorporate other cooperative instructional strategies—can provide contextual support to children who, like adults, are quick to recognize status groups and cliques.

- Create large, uninterrupted blocks of time for language-arts instruction, during which no children leave the room for special activities.

- Provide incentives to attract the very best teachers available and provide ongoing professional development, focusing on empowering teachers to make instructional decisions.

- Encourage ongoing professional development such as teacher networks that operate as voluntary support groups.

Given the perceived relationship between socioeconomic conditions and school achievement, school districts should address these incorrect assumptions to maximize the educational opportunities for all children. In the age of reform of urban school organizations, effective and significant focus on achievement is the primary measure of how schools and school leaders will be evaluated.

ADVANCED PLACEMENT AND LITERACY

Urban schools have consistently attempted to identify academic techniques that increase the performance of students. One of these techniques may not appear to be beneficial in urban environments has proven to be quite successful: advanced placement courses. In addition to advanced placement courses, literacy must be identified as a key ingredient for urban school success.

Advanced Placement Curriculum in Urban Schools. Placement models for urban education have been a part of the discussions regarding overall reforms dating back to the publication of *A Nation at Risk* in the 1983. The environment in which urban teachers and students learn is burdened with high levels of poverty, which have typically led to limited success in academic pursuits for most students (Clune, 1997). Another challenge for urban schools in terms of identifying advanced-placement academic programs is the high concentration of students with limited English skills (Duncombe, Ruggeriero, and Yinger, 1996). Advanced placement academic initiatives, Clune (1997) has identified eleven elements that must be addressed in order to help students achieve academic success in urban schools. The eleven elements that must be addressed are:

- ◆ Discontinue graduating urban high-school students who score minimally on achievement tests.
- ◆ Work in low-poverty schools and identify demographics components of all studies.
- ◆ Phase in pilot programs that directly influence student achievement.
- ◆ Collect data on student mobility.
- ◆ Define education technology to be used in accelerated programs.
- ◆ Evaluate areas of extra need and the costs of experimental programs, analyze spending and budgetary waste, and reallocate existing financial resources.
- ◆ Assess appropriate ways to structure state aid for the possible creation of a site-based funding formula for high-poverty schools.

♦ Determine how accelerated education can be implemented on a wide scale with the intention of attracting schools to join an accelerated-schools network to discover together the obstacles of implementation.

♦ Determine which government programs and structures are optimal and tolerable for accelerated education.

♦ Assess vouchers as a means to achieve accelerated education.

♦ Determine which agencies create and implement remedies for high-poverty schools and how stakeholders can identify a focused policy initiative at the state or national level.

The original intent of advanced-placement courses was to identify specifically gifted high-school students and assist them in securing college credit. When the program was created in 1955, there was limited participation throughout the country. According to Steller and Lambert (1996) there were only 1,200 AP exams administered in 1955 compared to 750,000 exams administered in 1995. The authors noted "the AP exams were administered to almost 500,000 high-school students representing approximately 11,000 high schools across the United States" (p. 97).

There is an interesting distinction regarding the interpretation of advanced-placement courses in urban schools. As suggested earlier, the stereotypical notion is that urban schools do not have students achieving at advanced academic levels. Steller and Lambert suggested, in their example of a new teacher in the Oklahoma City Public Schools, that while there were advanced-placement courses being offered at the high school, there were a limited number of students who performed at a sufficient level to secure college credit. As a result, there was attitudinal opposition to the idea of creating a process that had substance over style.

The process to re-evaluate Oklahoma City's advanced-placement program occurred and required "funding for teacher incentives, staff development, instructional materials and supplies, tutoring students, reducing the financial burdens placed on students, and student incentives in the form of college scholarships" (p. 99). Specifically, several guidelines were approved which provided structure and a format for the system. These guidelines have been deemed important for other urban districts considering advanced-placement programs. The guidelines included:

- Supplemental compensation earmarked for faculty members who teach AP courses.

- A year-end bonus for AP teachers based on student achievement on the AP examinations. (In the Oklahoma City Schools example, teachers would receive additional financial support for each student who scored at specific achievement levels.)

- AP teachers were required to attend an AP workshop of their choice.

- AP teachers would receive $15 dollar per hour for tutoring students before and after class.

- AP teachers would receive all of the instructional material, equipment, and textbooks required to teach AP courses.

- A national search was conducted specifically aimed at hiring AP teachers.

- The school district offered discounts for low-income students in order to register for AP examinations.

- AP students received college scholarships based on AP exam scores.

- An AP administrator was appointed to recruit teachers, provide guidance, and monitor the $250,000 allocated for the project.

In the Oklahoma City Public Schools and other urban districts throughout the country, there is a central question regarding whether urban students can achieve at high academic levels and to what degree they can compete with their peers from suburban and rural districts. Advanced-placement programs, like the one described above, have served as catalysts for academic engagement for both students and teachers in other urban communities. It is likely that parents and community activists support this type of program. These programs, however, require commitment from school stakeholders as well as strong student and parental support.

LITERACY ISSUES IN HIGH-POVERTY URBAN SCHOOLS

The need for urban parents from high-poverty communities to read to their children is key to school success. Parents are the central focus for literacy programs. Much of the research on literacy programs indicates a need to develop intergenerational programs that encourage literacy instruction for children and parents (Morrow, Tracy, and Maxwell, 1995; Morrow, 1995; and Elish-Piper, 1997). Understanding the home environment of young readers from urban environments is an important aspect to creating additional opportunities for success. The research indicates that children from middle-income and low-income homes receive different literacy assistance. Options available to middle-income families include computer access, visits to museums and other locations where reading activities are stressed. Some researchers concluded that "low income families used literacy for social, technical, and aesthetic purposes in daily lives" (Elish-Piper, p. 257).

One study conducted by Elish-Piper (1997) examined thirteen low-income urban families. These families participated in a nine-week, summer family-literacy pilot project. "The study sought to describe the literacy uses of these families, their responses to the program, and the program's development" (p. 257). The program had a specific focus for the nine weeks and included the following topics:

♦ television guides
♦ literacy games
♦ newspapers
♦ telephone books

- written directions
- storytelling
- book-making with families' stories
- expository children's literature
- narrative children's literature.

The results of the study indicated that all the urban families used literacy for meaningful and significant purposes, but differences existed in terms of social-contextual factors within each family. In other words, "life situations, goals, and needs of the families determined their need and uses for literacy" (p. 266).

Three other significant findings were identified by Elish-Piper. Children's literature may not always be the appropriate starting point for family-literacy programs. This finding is consistent with the premise that other factors influence the level of literacy engagement, such as resources, materials, and activities with which the family is knowledgeable and comfortable. The second significant finding suggested that families who developed ownership of the program experienced a high retention-rate. Packaged programs were discouraged. The third finding indicated that, due to the limited research in this area, the social-contextual approach for literacy development in urban schools and communities should continue to be investigated.

THE IMPORTANCE OF PARENTAL INVOLVEMENT

Benjamin Bloom (1980) has argued that parents may be the most important factor in promoting student achievement, simply because they are the most consistent figures in the child's life. Parental influence on children's intellectual development has been found in children as young as three months (Slaughter and Epps, 1987). A paper presented at the biennial meeting of the Society for Research in Child Development by Clark-Stewart, Blumenthal, and Caldwell (1985) noted that among children between the ages of 9 and 36 months, African-American children tended to advance in language development and showed a greater tendency to respond to stimulation by maternal verbal behaviors that are continually responsive to the child's speech behaviors. There are also indications of positive verbal and non-verbal behaviors reflective of active parental participation in the child's ongoing play. The researchers concluded that the value of verbal responsiveness, from the child's perspective, is not primarily intellectual, but social and emotional.

In essence, "parents are, in effect, the child's earliest teachers because they do, in their priorities, expectancies, and behaviors, influence the course of the child's achievement development" (Slaughter, 1989, p. 6). The general research on parental involvement is relatively clear. We know that better parental involvement improves student achievement and positive parental perceptions about schools is directly related to reducing school dropout rates, suspension, and failure.

Lightfoot (1988) has argued that both teachers and parents have images and stereotypes of one another that stem from their own childhood experiences and guide their view of what school is or should be for the children for whom they are responsible. Ogbu (1985) has stated that based on historical events relating to educational practices dating back to slavery, African-American parents have long had a crisis in confidence relating to the benefits of public education for their children. Ogbu noted than whenever a subcultural minority has historically experienced caste-like restrictions in legitimizing their existence, parents have difficulty supporting a family and family consistency is hindered severely. As a result of these caste restrictions, African-American children, especially boys, have learned that education is not a vehicle that leads to social mobility and opportunity. Thus they have developed negative attitudes toward school (Gibbs, 1988; Lightfoot, 1988; Wilson, 1989).

The importance of parental involvement to school success for African-Americans has been stressed by Bronfenbrenner (1978) in that:

♦ Parental involvement contributes to children's cognitive and affective development

♦ Intervention efforts with children are most effective when parents actively participate in those efforts

♦ The parent is the major vehicle by which the community can reach the child and family

- Linking the home and the school environment will be beneficial to parents, teachers, administrators, and especially children
- Parents are resources and thereby worthy of investment
- The family, not the school, provides the child with a primary source of values and behavioral reference points
- The uniqueness of the parent-child relationship as compared to teacher-child or peer-child relationships is critical to the success of the school in its relationship to the child.

It has been proposed that racial socialization by parents is critical to school success. For example, Bowman and Howard (1985) reported the results of a national survey of 317 African-American youths between the ages of 14 and 24. The study investigated the relationship between racial socialization by parents to the self-reported grades of respondents. The results indicated that grades were lowest for the one-third of the youths who reported that their parents had told them nothing about race relations in the United States. Youth socialized to be aware of racial barriers reported significantly higher grades. The authors concluded that "it is through an emphasis on ethnic pride, self-development, racial barriers, and egalitarianism that Black parents attempt to filter to the developing child the meaning of his/her racial status" (p. 136).

Powell (1982) concluded that parents and schools play a major role in communicating both expectations and encouragement for achievement. Powell suggested a number of ways to enhance self-esteem in African-American children and thereby improve their academic performance:

- Maximize participation by parents and children
- Reinforce mores, values of the home, the immediate family and the community and school

- Reflect African-American culture and lifestyles in the educational curriculum
- Encourage academic achievement regardless of social class

Schurr (1992) suggested sixteen practical measures that educators can use to enhance parental involvement in schools. She also suggested that administrators review and consider seven common elements identified by the Southwest Educational Development Laboratory in a study of promising parent involvement programs:

- A written policy that legitimizes the importance of parental involvement
- Administrative support represented by dollars, space, and people power
- Training focused on communication and partnering skills for parents and staff members
- Emphasis on a partnership philosophy that creates a feeling of mutual ownership in the education of students
- Two-way communication that occurs regularly and consistently
- Networking that facilitates the sharing of information, resources, and technical support
- Regular evaluation activities undertaken to modify program components as needed.

The sixteen proven ways to involve parents as identified by Schurr (1992) are as follows:

- Mutual goal setting, contracting, and evaluating
- Assessing school policies, practices, and rituals
- Providing a parent lounge/center/resource room

- Preparing public information displays, public service messages, and work-site seminars
- Publishing a parent handbook of guidelines and tips
- Holding a weekend or evening public information fair
- Organizing a parent and student exchange day
- Offering extra academic credit for parent involvement
- Hosting an old-fashioned family night at school
- Initiating a school-wide communication plan
- Establishing parent-teacher dialogue journals for communication
- Encourage official parent proclamation efforts
- Preparing and sending monthly home-achievement packets
- Scheduling home visits for a special bond
- Setting a school-wide homework policy
- Introducing a meet-and-greet program

School administrators in urban communities should use these suggestions and recognize parents as significant contributors and stakeholders with the school process. Aronson (1996) strongly recommends that schools clearly communicate with parents the expectation of parental involvement in the educational process. As an example, one of the contemporary techniques being used by school districts is the use of technology to communicate with parents. A number of schools currently use automatic dialing systems to call parents and introduce new services to the school. Schools are also using this simple technology to encourage teachers and administrators to leave messages regarding class activities for children or simply as a means to communicate with each other. Bausch (1990) described a similar technology program used to communicate with parents in a Nashville, Tennessee, school district. The program has met with good success.

A recent review of the literature pertaining to parental involvement and academic success consistently confirms previous research that parental involvement in education remains one of the most significant positive variables in increasing student achievement (Gullatt, 1997). In addition to parental involvement, students facing tremendous adversity who ascertain that they are part of a positive and caring environment will likely increase their work ethic and ultimately enjoy the school experience to a greater degree (Epstein, 1995). Urban parents can particularly benefit from community partnerships that focus on parental involvement and school interaction. Epstein contends that when schools provide a nurturing environment with rigorous, fair academic programs combined with effective parental communication, success is likely to occur.

Urban school leaders must go beyond the traditional open-house as the primary means of communicating and interacting with parents. Davies (1996) suggests that effective educational leaders create school activities that encourage parents to become participants in activities in addition to drama and sporting events typically held at the school. It has been noted that the teachers typically want to talk with parents concerning their children but these parents typically do not attend open-houses or drama presentations.

A number of professionals have often remarked that the parents who attend open-houses cannot wait to hear what they already know, which is how well their children are doing. Many parents who have not had successful or enjoyable school experiences do not attend school, because they do not want to be reminded that they are failures or lack sufficient parenting skills. Often the parents feel that the success or failure of their children is a direct reflection of their parenting skills.

Current Themes in Parental Involvement

Much of the current discussions on parental involvement is centered around several themes, namely that parental involvement in curriculum matters; that schools must work to empower and recruit parents to participate; and that parents' authority should be included in school decision-making.

Successful school reform movements must actively engage parents in their improvement efforts. The importance of parental involvement and their influence on student learning is rapidly becoming a contemporary issue for all school organizations.

Swick and Broadway (1997) indicate that parental self-image and the ability to control life's interactions, adaptations to the changes in life, and interpersonal resources are factors that not only affect the quality, but also the amount of parental involvement in schools. These factors all play roles in the degree of influence parents exert on children's learning process. Educators should be sensitive to these factors but also aware of the complexities of parental influence.

Parenting can be difficult and stressful. Parenting becomes even more difficult when life choices are complicated by severe social, economic, and basic survival issues. Parents in urban environments are particularly susceptible to economic challenges that cause interactions with schools to be more difficult. Understanding urban parents and their experience with control provides some insight to school leaders about the attitudes and dispositions parents have when they arrive at school. Parents who are externally controlled typically leave the activities at school up to teachers and administrators (Swick and Broadway, 1997). Parents from urban environments are extremely interested in their children succeeding and doing well. Urban parents tend to depend on the school to provide them with information about how their children can succeed in life.

Meyer, Delargardelle, and Middleton (1997) described the Ames Community (Iowa) School District's design for an innovative middle-school mathematics curriculum to elicit parent support and ease anxiety. The primary goal of the new curriculum was to shift from a traditional perspective in mathematics to a program designed to make mathematics more flexible through problem solving. The plan was developed to respond to anticipated parental concerns about curriculum development in general and mathematics competencies in particular. The school leadership in Ames used six general strategies to engage parents in the school curriculum matters:

- Being confident with the program or policy
- Treating parents as equal partners
- Being honest with parents
- Defining accountability and specific responsibilities of the school

- Communicating effectively
- Selecting support people carefully

A second current trend in parental involvement centers on empowering and recruiting parents to become active in school matters. While there is common agreement among researchers and practitioners about the need to empower parents, there has been more discussion recently about how involved parents should really be in the school. Clemens-Brower (1997) has outlined four strategies for getting parents and community members involved in the school process. These techniques used by school organizations are investing in a voice mail system, inviting people to share their experiences, obtaining assistance in gathering information for lesson plans, and creating monthly learning celebrations.

A third parental involvement trend involves parental decision-making and how schools can create a comfortable working relationship with parents. Dodd (1998) reported there is evidence to suggest that as children advance to junior high and high school, there is limited engagement of parents in the school. Some of the reasons parents tend to disengagement with schools and their children's activities in school include the following: (a) teenagers' express negative attitudes toward parental involvement; (b) parents feel their educational experiences were less than positive; and (c) parents are unsure whether teachers really "understand" them (Dodd, 1998).

The challenge for urban school leaders is to determine to what degree parents should be involved in decision-making. Some school leaders may view parental involvement as a threat to school policy and implementation. All school stakeholders need to ensure there is common ground for all participants.

BARRIERS TO AND TECHNIQUES FOR EFFECTIVE INVOLVEMENT FOR URBAN PARENTS

The literature is quite specific regarding barriers for urban parents and their schools. Here is a list of typical issues urban parents confront:

♦ Previous Negative School Interactions. While this is not a revelation, it is worth mentioning again. School leaders must realize that a number of parents experienced negative interactions at school during their own school years. As a result, coming to the school for any reason brings about anxiety and tension. Often this anxiety and tension result in negative communication between urban parents and school personnel.

♦ Communication Style and Approach. The manner in which communication occurs between urban parents and school personnel is critical to continued parental involvement. At some urban schools it is quite apparent that parents are not welcomed visitors. For example, at some schools parents are required to wait for long periods before their questions are answered and they are rarely referred to by name. With all of the socioeconomic difficulties that impact their lives, urban parents often rely heavily on the school for "doing the right thing" for the educational development of their children. However, these negative messages in the school environment become yet another way that urban parents are discouraged and disempowered from making a positive difference in the lives of their children. When school personnel send the message that parents are disruptions, feelings of alienation emerge, which further inhibits parental empowerment and involvement in the school. Furthermore, the parent then intentionally or unintentionally communicates negative messages to the child about educational achievement. Reducing alienation and including parents become salient issues, particularly as research (Henderson, 1987) has indicated that the relationship between parents and school personnel is linked to student academic achievement. Despite the plight of urban parents and the multiple difficulties that urban school personnel experience, there is a need to develop and maintain positive school-parent liaisons if urban children are to succeed in school.

- Family Composition. Urban families are not unlike other families in American society in terms of change and transition. The changing family structure in urban communities makes it critical for school personnel to research and plan effective programming for urban parents. This research should undertake learning parental work schedules, involving other community institutions, and providing day-care facilities when parents visit the school.

- Transportation. Although it is not the school's responsibility to provide transportation to parents, in order to facilitate involvement and interaction schools could arrange for parent-teacher interaction to take place in central areas. Thus planned, parents could easily walk to the meeting place to discuss their children's educational achievement with teachers, counselors, and administrators.

- Attitude Toward Urban Parents. The media might have us believe that all urban schools operate like the school portrayed in the popular movie "Lean On Me." Fortunately, an overwhelming majority of urban schools are managed efficiently and are safe, but this does not necessarily change the attitude toward urban parents exhibited by some urban school personnel. Urban parents must be viewed as stakeholders and participants in the school organization.

Some of the techniques for involving urban parents include the following recommendations:

- Empower Urban Parents. The term "empower" is perhaps a bit overused in educational circles, but urban parents genuinely need to be active participants in a shared vision for the school. If there is a genuine interest in creating urban schools that work, then parents must not just attend an occasional PTA meeting; they must be involved in policy and goal attainment within the school.

♦ Avoid the "Joe Clark" Syndrome. This recommendation suggests not waiting until the school and parental interaction is so negative that school boards and
other governing bodies will accept any kind of interaction or management within the school. Difficult
issues must be addressed and resolved in mutually
beneficial ways. The central theme in this recommendation is to make restructuring school and empowering parents priorities. Do not wait for a state
department of education or a federal educational
agency to take over the school. Action should be taken
when problems arise. Waiting without a plan of action should be unacceptable. While this may be "easier
said than done," all decisions should be centered on
what is in the best interest of children in the school.

♦ Establish Family-School Partnerships. Successful urban schools will use every opportunity to involve parents in the school process. Parent-teacher aides,
monitors, and involvement in planning are proven
techniques that encourage parental participation.

♦ Involve Parents in School Planning and Organization.
When urban parents truly feel part of the overall planning and development of their schools, it leads to enhanced community involvement. Jesse (1996)
emphasized the importance of having a shared vision
with parents to encourage effective parental involvement.

The National Parent Teacher Association (1997) has identified six levels, or standards, of parental involvement, primarily
based on Epstein's six types of parental involvement. These standards include:

♦ Communicating: home and school communication is
regular, two-way, and meaningful.

♦ Parenting: Parenting skills are promoted and sponsored.

♦ Student Learning: Parents play an integral role in assisting student learning.

♦ Volunteering: Parents are welcomed in the school, and their support and assistance are sought.

♦ School Decision-Making and Advocacy: Parents are full partners in the decisions that affect children and families.

♦ Collaboration with Community: Community resources are used to strengthen schools, families, and student learning.

It is important for urban parents to believe that school officials are sincere about their interaction with them and that open and honest, two-way communication indeed occurs in the school environment. The degree of open communication between urban school teachers and administrators will serve as the foundation for success of the children. In addition to open communication, a structured and organized instructional approach to parenting is a major aspect of involving parents. Having parenting classes at the school can also provide another opportunity for the teachers and parents to interact.

Student learning and the extent to which students experience success at school are vital aspects of parental involvement. Urban parents must be engaged in the academic lives of their children. Small activities, such as having a parent sign a letter or grade card, have only minimal success. Schools should create procedures where parents are required and encouraged to attend school on a regular basis to communicate with the school personnel about instructional activities they can do in the home. Schools can also be kept open for a period after the school day has ended in order to allow for additional academic work between parents and the child.

SUMMARY

There is a commonly held belief that as children advance in grades, parental involvement and volunteerism diminish. This may be particularly true for parents of children who have not been successful in school. Parental volunteering begins with an open and welcoming environment to parents. I visited an elementary school where there was a sign on the front door of the school that read "Parents—Stay Out." Upon inquiry, I learned from the principal that he had experienced some problems with parents who had come to school before the end of the day and who took their children out of class without going through the appropriate procedures. I shared with the principal that while I could appreciate his concern for child safety, he should also be concerned about what message this sends to parents who pick their children up on time and read this sign upon entering the school. Parent volunteers are important and should be sought out for support for the school.

Much of the school restructuring information suggests that parents need to play a more significant role in the decision-making procedures in schools. While the notion of parental decision-making might be objectionable to school administrators and teachers, there is a need for parents not only to be perceived as stakeholders, but also to be included in decision-making situations where their stakeholder role is validated. This degree of involvement is a major shift for some school leaders. It requires trust and compromise by parents and urban school personnel.

If there is a central theme to Epstein's (1995) six standards of parental involvement, it is the strand that emphasizes collaboration and community resources as a means of building schools and families. The resources are primarily human resources combined with capital from the school and businesses in the community. This approach calls for a radical approach to school funding and authority—permitting individual schools to receive directly the property tax revenue or the funds provided by state departments of education. This type of grass-roots decision-making would involve the resources coming directly to the school for collaboration between the school, families, and community at large.

Daniels (1996) has suggested that few schools genuinely involve parents in decision-making regarding curriculum and other policy related issues. Some urban school teachers and administrators believe that urban parents do not have the appropriate skills to participate in a structured decision-making process. The existence of this view is supported by Wadsworth (1997), who completed a study that clearly indicated that the American public was angry, frustrated, and exhibited little confidence in the future of educational leadership in public schools. There is sufficient argument that the public's view of urban education is even more dismal than the view of non-urban school environments.

Another variable considered critical for urban students to become academically successful is the presence of appropriate role models (Busby and Barnett, 1986; Cooper, 1989; Irvine, 1990a; Matthews and Odom, 1989; Merchant, 1990; Ogbu, 1985). Researchers have suggested that African-American children need significant role models in order to develop and sustain their black identities (Edmonds, 1979; Hale, 1989; Lyons, 1990; White and Parham, 1984). Positive role models, especially esteemed African-American teachers, help counterbalance negative role models prevalent in many African-American communities (Busby and Barnett, 1986). By seeing the benefits of educational attainment apparent in the participation of black teachers and professors, African-American students can be more easily encouraged to pursue positive careers and become productive citizens of their communities.

Locke (1989) set forth some general guidelines to help educators foster positive images in African-American children. They are as follows:

♦ Plan to be open and honest in relationships with African-American children. Leave yourself open to culturally different attitudes and encourage African-American children to be open and honest with you about issues related to their culture.

♦ Learn as much as possible about your own culture. One can appreciate another culture more, if there is first an appreciation of one's own culture.

♦ Seek to respect genuinely and appreciate culturally different attitudes and behaviors. Demonstrate that you both recognize and value the African-American culture.

♦ Take advantage of all available opportunities to participate in activities in the African-American community in your school and community throughout the
   year.

♦ Keep in mind that African-American children are both
   members of their unique cultural group and are unique
   individuals as well. Strive to keep a healthy balance
   between your view of students as cultural beings and
   as unique beings.

♦ Eliminate behaviors that suggest prejudice or racism
   and do not tolerate such behaviors from your colleagues or from children themselves.

♦ Encourage teachers and administrators in your school
   to institutionalize practices that acknowledge African-
   American culture.

♦ Hold high expectations for African-American children
   and encourage all who work with African-American
   children to do likewise.

♦ Ask questions about African-American culture and
   learn as much as possible. Share this information with
   your colleagues.

♦ Develop culturally-specific strategies, mechanisms,
   techniques, and programs to foster the psychological
   development of African-American children.

A substantial majority of white student teachers and beginning administrators tend to identify themselves as "American"
without understanding the significance of ethnic identification
and knowledge. From a historical perspective, white ethnic
groups were pressured, through the Americanization process,
to assimilate into American society by eliminating all identification (e.g., ethnic languages and values) with their ethnic groups.
The term American initially became consciously synonymous
with being white. However, in more recent years (particularly
during the Black Power and Civil Rights Movement) African-
Americans have challenged the perception of being American,
meaning white, by maintaining their ethnic group identifica-

tion and struggling to be recognized as Americans with full citizenship rights. In essence, whites (e.g., teachers, counselors, and administrators) are often unfamiliar with ethnic group membership and identification and may unconsciously still view being American with being white. They do not understand why minority groups insist upon maintaining their ethnic group identification.

If school leaders are going to provide positive images, they must eliminate behaviors that suggest prejudice or racism. School leaders must not tolerate such behaviors in colleagues nor in the children themselves. Through racial socialization in the general society, their cultural community and families, and the school environment, many urban students become quite adept at recognizing subtle racism and/or classism in cross-cultural relationships at school. Consequently, it is critical that school personnel examine themselves for holding cultural biases, harboring stereotypes, and for making assumptions about underrepresented, low-income children of poverty. Despite politically correct behavior the teacher, administrator, or staff member might harbor negative feelings and beliefs about urban students that are eventually revealed in language, facial expressions, decisions, and overall behavior toward these students.

The success or failure of effective educational programming for urban students suggests to educators and policymakers that a correlation exists between positive educational programming and successful urban students.

3

DEBATING SELF-ESTEEM AND URBAN STUDENTS

INTRODUCTION

Self-esteem has been defined as the way a person feels about oneself. This includes the degree to which one possesses self-respect and self-acceptance (Glassman, 1988). The literature often presents varied and conflicting views of the relationship between self-esteem and achievement. However, Black (1991) indicated that there have been more than twenty terms used to define the meaning of self-esteem. He pointed out that "the imprecise terminology contributes to confusion, misunderstanding, and misapplication of findings" (p. 28).

There has been a somewhat significant debate about the difference between self-esteem and self-concept. Beane (1991) suggested that self-concept is viewed as the aspects of one's self-image that are basically descriptive and non-judgmental, whereas self-esteem is construed as those aspects or attitudes that are classified as self-evaluative. Essentially, Scott, Murray, Mertens, and Dustin (1996) posit that the distinction between self-esteem and self-concept is significant and that the evaluative aspect is likely to be impacted by a person's values and environment. Without question, the impact of self-esteem and self-concept on underrepresented populations within educational institutions is a major issue among all the challenges that confront these populations.

A REVIEW OF SELF-ESTEEM

Esteem needs were first studied in depth by Abraham Maslow. In his book, *Motivation and Personality*, Maslow reported ways that self-esteem relates to the process of becoming a self-actualized person. According to Maslow, "all people have a need or desire for a stable, firmly based, sense of self-regard, or self-respect, and they need the esteem from themselves and others" (Maslow, 1970, p. 78). Maslow identified two categories of esteem needs. The first category of esteem needs includes the desire for strength, achievement, adequacy, mastery, competence, self-confidence, and a degree of independence and freedom. The second category of esteem needs involves the desire for prestige, status, recognition, attention, dignity, and appreciation. All of these needs are characteristics of esteem based on others' views of the person (Maslow, 1970).

Stanley Coopersmith (1967) concluded that high self-esteem results from parental acceptance, the setting of limits, and freedom for individual action within realistic limits. Coopersmith also found other significant factors related to self-esteem. Among these factors are religion, social class, ethnic group, and traumatic experiences in childhood. However, Coopersmith viewed the quality and amount of parental attention and acceptance one receives in childhood as critical antecedents to the development of one's self-esteem.

Much of the initial research regarding self-esteem and the achievement levels of students was conducted specifically examining the differences between African-American students and white students. While all underrepresented groups have a unique culture and value system, much of the emphasis in the literature is concerned with African-American self-esteem issues. Caution should be exercised when attempting to generalize self-esteem issues to all underrepresented groups. Many of the examples in this chapter will look at self-esteem from an African-American perspective; however many of the patterns and issues are fairly consistent among underrepresented groups.

Kenneth B. Clark (1939, 1947) completed two of the early studies relating to the self-esteem of African-American students. In his 1939 study, Clark examined 150 African-American children from five Works Progress Administration nursery schools in the Washington, D.C., area. Clark used a standard picture test of forced choice between photographs of black and white boys to determine racial identification. The results of his study indicated that race consciousness and racial identification are indicative of particular self-consciousness by obvious physical characteristics.

Clark's 1947 study has come to be known as the famous "doll test." Clark surveyed 253 African-American children ages three through seven. One hundred-thirty-four of the children were from segregated schools, and 119 were from northern racially mixed schools. The dolls in the test, one black and one white, were used to identify color and desirability. Some examples of the questions used were:" Can you give me the doll you want to play with? Can you give me the doll that looks bad? Can you give me the doll that is a nice color? (Clark, 1947, p. 63).

The results of this study were interpreted to indicate self-negation and self-depreciation on the part of African-American children. Findings of this study also confirmed that children can correctly identify racial differences. Although white children made more correct racial self-identifications, the most significant finding was that African-American children preferred white to colored dolls.

Another related study was conducted by Radke, Sutherland, and Rosenberg (1960) with African-American and white children, ages seven through thirteen in grades two through six. Subjects included a total of 475 African-American students and 46 white students in a low socioeconomic area of Pittsburgh where seventy-five percent to eighty-five percent of the population was African-American. Subjects were asked to respond to a picture test consisting of thirty-two photos (eight of African-American boys, eight African-American girls, eight white boys, and eight white girls) projected on a screen on slides of eight pictures each. Twelve common stereotypes of blacks such as lazy, dull, dishonest, etc., were used to formulate descriptions that were used in the test. Respondents were asked to select pictures of the children who demonstrated certain characteristics. Examples included items such as: Which child comes to school clean? Which three children in the picture would you like to have as friends? Which three would you not like to have as friends? Results of this study indicated that African-Americans assigned undesirable characteristics to black pictures. Also, in the choice of friends, only nine percent of the younger and twelve percent of the older children selected black pictures. Slightly more than half the rejections of both blacks and whites were of black pictures. Whites in all situations and all ages expressed strong preference for their own racial group, particularly when choices between blacks and whites as friends were on an abstract or wish level. On assignment of behavior characteristics to their own race and to whites, African-Americans showed a much less positive attitude toward the white race. But, like whites, African-Americans showed readiness to assign undesirable characteristics to African-Americans. The researchers pointed out that what seemed to be self-rejection and ambivalence toward their own race appeared also in African-American responses to photos on questions of preferred friends. Responses of sixth-grade African-Americans, however, indicated more acceptance of their own race than did younger African-Americans, a finding that the researchers believed reflected rebellion against acceptance of derogatory stereotypes of African-Americans.

SELF-ESTEEM AND ACADEMIC ACHIEVEMENT

Crain, Mahard, and Narot (1982) investigated two aspects of academic success: achievement and self-esteem. These researchers found that most students felt reasonably good about their academic abilities and African-Americans were as confident as whites, despite generally low test scores and grades. This study also revealed that for African-American males feelings about school race-relations were critical to their ability to do school work well, whereas for whites, school race-relations were not a primary concern regarding their ability to become successful in school. The researchers found that racial tension rose when interracial contact was highest. However, the researchers also found that African-American male students in predominately black schools had higher self-esteem than African-American girls. They concluded that for African-Americans, and especially African-American males, achievement and self-esteem are strongly affected by the racial climate of the school. The investigators also noted that a knowledge of black history, lifestyle, and culture had a positive effect on African-American self-esteem. Results of some recent studies, however, have suggested that African-American students do not lack self-esteem.

For example, a study by White and Parham (1984) proposed that the self-concept and self-esteem of African-American students is a reflection of black life and the group's caste-like position in a dominant society. The researchers took the position that the notion of black children having a low self-concept should be discarded even though, "black Americans are incapable of rejecting the negativistic image of themselves" (p. 92). The notion of black children having a low self-concept was also questioned by Ford (1985) in reporting on his study of junior-high, inner-city schools located in low- and moderate- income neighborhoods. Results of Ford's study suggested that the overall self-esteem was high and that males were high in self-acceptance, self-security, and self-assertion. Females scored high in social confidence, peer affiliation, and teacher affiliation. Ford concluded that the view that inner-city black males have negative self-concepts and low self-esteem has "virtually developed into a stereotype and while this view might have been verified several years ago, the results of this study suggests this may no longer be the case" (p. 88).

As you would imagine, there are two sides to the argument of the value of self-esteem and its relationship to academic achievement. Alfie Kohn (1994) provided a comprehensive view of the lack of sufficient evidence to support a relationship between self-esteem and academic achievement. Kohn notes "the empirical evidence once again offers meager support for what seems intuitively indisputable" (p. 275). Kohn refers to at least three distinct reasons why he is cautious to declare affirmative views on the relationship between self-esteem and academic achievement: (1) the extent of the relationship is not impressive for a review of 128 studies on self-esteem; (2) the correlation between self-esteem and academic achievement is lower based on more contemporary studies; and (3) the need not only to research "a global measure of self-esteem (how positively they feel about themselves in general) [and] something more specific like academic self-esteem or even self-esteem regarding the ability to succeed at a particular subject" (p. 274). Essentially Kohn suggests that the range of significance at which major studies have suggested this relationship between self-esteem and academic achievement is not significant enough to substantiate a correlation. Kohn noted that the range of significance was only about four percent to seven percent variation.

Kohn (1994) summarizes his view of self-esteem by indicating that the data collected on self-esteem is essentially disappointing for several reasons:

- No one has shown that self-esteem does not matter. "The burden of proof would seem to rest with those arguing that our education system ought to be attending to a given factor" (p. 276).

- Self-esteem is related to things other than academic performance and social behavior. Kohn notes "depression and other psychological problems are highly correlated with low self-esteem. Once again, though, there is some disagreement about which causes which" (p. 276).

- Self-esteem may not be sufficient to produce achievement or to serve as a social vaccine, but it may be a necessary component.

- There is concern regarding the manner in which measurements are made and the ultimate relationship of a specific study to the importance of self-esteem.

Kohn also posits that other significant points focus on political implications of studies on self-esteem and potential social change, such as the focus of individualism versus community perspective on self-esteem, and the suggestion that those who are critical of self-esteem programs are slanted toward political conservatism. Perhaps a statement that best summarizes Kohn's perspective is "lurking just below the surface of critics polemics is the fear that somebody is going to get a free lunch" (p. 279).

In addition to the previously mentioned studies, Atherley (1990) concluded in her study of three schools between children with low academic ability and low socioeconomic status that "no support was found for the existence of positive relationships between academic ability alone and self-esteem between schools, but strong support was given to the hypothesis which suggested that within schools children of higher ability would have higher levels of self-esteem" (p. 225).

This study by Atherley (1990) and a subsequent study by Scott et al. (1996) provide excellent summaries on the value of self-esteem and academic achievement. It seems obvious that as far as underrepresented populations are concerned, there is a clear need for teachers, administrators, and guidance counselors to provide wholesome and psychologically healthy environments for these students who use education as a means of survival. Scott, et al. (1996) conclude their article by offering valuable implications for practice adapted from the California Task Force to Promote Self-esteem and Personal and Social Responsibility:

♦ Intertwine self-esteem and responsibility into the total educational program.

♦ Educate every educator—through preservice and inservice training—in self-esteem and responsibility.

♦ Give students opportunities to do community service.

♦ Formulate a real-life skills curriculum.

♦ Promote more parental involvement.

♦ Be sensitive to the needs of students at risk of failure.

♦ Use the arts to help develop self-esteem and responsibility.

♦ Expand counseling and peer-counseling services for students.

♦ Provide cooperative learning opportunities.

♦ Reduce class size or student-adult ratio.

♦ Implement programs to counteract bigotry and prejudice (p. 292).

SELF-ESTEEM AND PERSONAL RESPONSIBILITY

Because self-esteem and personal and social responsibility must be woven into the entire educational environment, all individuals in the school must participate and take responsibility for comprehensive improvement. Several questions arise. What does social responsibility encompass? How would teachers, administrators, and counselors encourage the development of self-esteem?

Urban school leaders need to identify methods to reinforce high academic achievement and thus healthy self-esteem by sponsoring students and encouraging them to participate in cultural events. The creation of rituals and symbols of community are essential to build self-esteem and social responsibility. Contributions from alumni and fundraising activities can also enhance a community-style self-esteem that will benefit children and help them feel positive about their school. Ultimately, the message that must be sent and received is that academic achievement is valued by the school and community.

Building self-esteem and social-responsibility could easily include various activities and programs within the school. Bulletin boards with pictures of graduates who are now in college would also boost esteem. One positive activity that many urban schools use is the "college day," where students who are in college come back to their school community (elementary or high school) and present to their peers their college experiences. These students can also model the "giving back" value of social responsibility, which can reflect very positively on the urban community.

Resources should be made available for every educator in urban schools to enhance and reinforce energies through staff development and inservice training in self-esteem and social responsibility. Inservice training and workshops should be interactive and require educators to become actively engaged in process and decision-making. Urban school leaders could become more familiar with strategies and approaches used by other school districts across the country. Urban leaders could also benefit and enhance the self-esteem and social responsibility of students by interacting with students in ways that show concern, respect, and understanding.

Students from urban communities are confronted with a number of challenges (including circular hopelessness discussed in chapter 1) and require urban school leaders to be knowledgeable about the culture, values, and norms of underrepresented populations. One of the reasons immersion schools were created resulted from an effort to provide professionals who would demonstrate concern, respect, and understanding as well as enhance self-esteem and social responsibility. Effective evaluations should also be in place in order to avoid the perception that the activities are a one-time event and not important after the workshop has concluded.

METHODS FOR ENHANCING SELF-ESTEEM

Although there is a legal debate about whether students should be required to do community service, some contend that community service activities build self-esteem and social responsibility. Providing opportunities for students to be actively involved in their community through the school programs seems beneficial. Students are able to provide a measure of commitment to their community and receive credit and recognition for their work at school. Also within the school context, urban students could benefit from a curriculum that identifies such skills as stress management, anger control, career planning, and other human relation skills. The school counseling units could provide beneficial special training opportunities for underrepresented students to learn critical-thinking and social skills for higher education and/or entering the world of work.

Urban leaders are already aware of the important role parents play in student success and the overall culture and climate of the school. However, it is essential that school personnel develop unique and innovative methods for attracting urban parents to the school. There is no substitute for the human touch and personal contact with people. Urban parents need to hear that their children can be successful in schools. Programs and workshops that highlight the importance of parents in the school are beneficial. We must find ways to empower urban parents. The point is simple: we already know that urban students need parental involvement. The challenge is for urban school districts to inspire parents to help their children do well in school, which will lead to higher self-esteem and subsequently higher academic achievement.

It is important for universities and urban school districts to develop a reciprocal working relationship. One idea for establishing reciprocity is to create a phone bank staffed by university students majoring in sales, counseling, education, and ethnic studies. The phone caller would solicit support for urban schools. The learning process would be beneficial for the college students in terms of gaining some hands-on experience in their chosen field of work and their work would provide a direct benefit for children in urban schools. Educators must learn to be more collaborative and respectful toward each other rather than allow their egos to get in the way of helping our children. As underrepresented urban populations remain uneducated, unemployed, imprisoned, and as these people are literally dying in the streets, we are squabbling about who is the best "qualified" to help. This refusal to collaborate from an inter-institutional perspective makes our preaching to low-income poverty students about the value of working together seem very hollow at a minimum; or worse, it makes us educated hypocrites.

Another way to enhance self-esteem and social responsibility is through the receipt of grants used to increase social support that could provide salaries and consultants' fees for qualified social workers, counselors, school psychologists, and other professionals to provide group classes on parenting skills, social-skill development, and short-term training programs for employment skills. Self-esteem and social responsibility could be enhanced by making day-care facilities available on campus for parents who serve as teachers' aides. Support for these grants must come from local, state, and national efforts.

Yet another method for enhancing self-esteem and social responsibility is using the arts. Creativity is a wonderful way for allowing urban children to think and grow in ways that are new and exciting. Involvement in the arts increases self-esteem by providing students an opportunity to be on stage, learn communication, work in teams, and practice social skills. Exposure to museums and university galleries allows a more global experience outside their local community.

Urban school districts are encouraged to expand the role of counselors and peer-counseling services for students. Perhaps we should look at the feasibility of allowing school counselors to provide critical counseling services for troubled youths in school rather than maintaining them as paper pushers who are often responsible for hundreds of students in a school. There are budgetary constraints, but there always seems to be money in the budget for prisons. It is interesting to note that when African-American boys get into trouble, there is always enough money for a jail cell, but when they need support, we cannot seem to find financial resources to address their needs before prisons enter the picture.

USING DIVERSITY TRAINING TO IMPACT SELF-ESTEEM

In addition to small classes, urban schools should implement programs to counteract bigotry and prejudice. The best approach is to provide consistent cultural-diversity training for all school personnel. When school personnel are not only sensitive but aware of social, cultural, and value-related issues for students, self-esteem will likely be affected in a positive manner. Patterson-Stewart (1999) has noted the following:

Cultural diversity training should be based on the premise that the United States is a heterogeneous society and our institutions of learning must prepare our children for effective citizenship in a multicultural world. Consequently, it is critical for educators and support personnel to learn teaching and helping concepts and behaviors that provide our children with the maximum opportunities for learning and achievement in a pluralistic society. The content and process activities should reflect the research and perspectives of noted authorities in the field of multicultural education and counseling and serve as a guide toward multicultural competence.

Patterson-Stewart (1999) suggests that cultural diversity training could be divided into four distinct components of learning that include awareness of self as a cultural being, which includes approaches to diversity and an examination of values and belief systems. The second component focuses on knowledge about the cycle and dynamics of oppression and racial identity development. The third component identifies multicultural competencies of educators and the school staff. The final component calls for putting all of these aspects together in a celebration and commitment to cultural diversity.

It is apparent that continuing dialogue and debate is necessary in order to effectively implement self-esteem programs in urban schools. We constantly talk about the needs and demands on educators and schools for the twenty-first century. We recognize that the world is changing, and if the world is changing, so are the preparation and support needs of urban children—especially African-American males.

African Americans and Self-Esteem

One of the most comprehensive studies of self-esteem among African-Americans was conducted by Coleman (1966) and involved a survey of 640,000 pupils. This study measured children's sense of control over their environment. It revealed that African-American children with high self-esteem as well as high interest in school had a lower sense of environmental control than white children.

In most studies conducted about African-Americans and self-esteem, some reference to socioeconomic status is likely to occur. This relationship is inevitable because of the nature of interactions African-Americans experience within the social, economic, and political structures of American culture. There is a widely held belief by personnel that the behavior problems children exhibit in schools are related to the idea that these children do not have high self-esteem and genuinely feel badly about themselves. A learning theory proposed by Bandura (1977) posited that the self-esteem exhibited by parents would be reflected in their children. In contrast to the view that children have no role in their degree of self-esteem provided to them by parents is the position supported by Atherley (1990) which concludes the "Mirroring" theory is more appropriate. The "Mirroring" theory contends that self-esteem attributes are related to psychological concerns as opposed to purely socioeconomic realities. Atherley believes that in addition to parents, the child's self-esteem is significantly impacted by the attitude of teachers toward children.

Atherly's findings are supported by a study Sanders (1992) conducted. This study of African-American males in a large Midwestern elementary school revealed that the degree of self-esteem was closely related to students' attitudes toward school and their perception of their own intellectual achievement. The study revealed that African-American males in the schools believed the attitude of the principal and the teachers played a significant role in the behaviors of the boys. From this study comes the example of a principal who was so popular with students that it was impossible for him to even walk down the hall because literally every student in the building wanted to interact with him, especially the African-American males. In fact, this principal would cause such a disruption when he walked through the cafeteria during lunch, because students would want to talk with him and literally follow him around the cafeteria that teachers supervising the lunchroom asked him not to come to the cafeteria during lunch. Mr. Henry, the principal, demonstrated several qualities that enabled him to have an impact on the attitudes and behaviors of students in his building. Mr. Henry was warm and clearly demonstrated concern about the students. He referred to students by name, asked about their relatives by name, and asked students to give messages to parents or relatives. Mr. Henry interacted positively with his staff. Teachers, cooks, and custodians greeted him with a warm smile when he approached them. Mr. Henry demonstrated the kind of skills necessary for every urban principal across the country. These skills included a genuine concern for the students in his building, quality leadership skills, strong communication skills, knowledge of the culture, values, and norms of the school and community, involvement of parents in school decision making, and a sense of ownership of the building and future of the children. When interacting with Mr. Henry, one felt good about being at school. Students are likely to become high achievers when the conditions of the school are such that success becomes an expectation rather than a dream.

A similar group of African-American males in another elementary school did not have this degree of interaction with their principal. This principal's was somewhat cold and distant. It was apparent that the students had a different response to this leadership approach. It would also be logical to assume that the nature of this interaction would have some impact on student's self-esteem and their attitude about teachers and the school as a whole. In other words, a principal and teacher who demonstrate negative leadership qualities will impact the self-esteem of children in the building and subsequently have a negative impact on academic achievement.

Another study related to African-American self-esteem was conducted by Matthews and Odom (1989). They examined elementary students in a predominately black school. Results of this study indicated that low levels of anxiety are associated moderately with high levels of self-esteem. These researchers supported findings by Ford's (1985) and Battle's (1987) studies, in which they indicated that black children, especially males, have high levels of self-esteem, even though scholastic and achievement data would suggest that such levels of high self-esteem might not be warranted. In other words, students in urban schools reported having high self-esteem, but their academic performance did not warrant them having such a high regard for themselves and their future.

In contrast, an earlier study by Lay and Wakstein (1985) suggested that high grades and high test scores are associated with high self-esteem for both black and white children. And Mboya (1986) found a significant positive relationship between self-concept of academic ability and academic achievement among black students. Mboya noted: "Black children's orientation toward school is different from the way they feel about themselves, meaning Black adolescents may view academic achievement as a separate activity which does not influence greatly their personal feelings of self" (p. 694).

In schools, the movement to build students' self-esteem can be traced back to the 1960s (Beane, 1991). Concern about self-esteem evolved into an actual movement that resulted in many school districts incorporating the value of enhancing self-esteem and the positive relationship with academic achievement into their goals and objectives. Beane (1991) saw three reasons why school districts began to emphasize the importance of enhancing students' self-esteem: (1) the expanding role of the school as a social agency that attempts to contribute to the general health

and well-being of students; (2) the increasing focus on participation, completion, self-direction and various other skills as factors considered significant in the development of young people;
and (3) the increasing concern for the students' personal effectiveness or power and whether students feel that such can make
a difference.

An interesting study by Wood, Hillman, and Sawilowsky
(1996) was conducted with 117 African-American adolescents
defined as at-risk. Their families were below the poverty line.
The young people in this study shared four major issues: (a)
their families were below the poverty line; (b) their reading and
math scores on the California Achievement Test were below
grade levels; (c) they were 14 or 15 years old; and (d) they were
referred by the school psychologist, social worker, or counselor
as being at-risk for dropping out of school (p. 599). The adolescents in this study completed self-concept and self-esteem inventories. The researchers concluded that even though children
came from similar social and economic conditions (in this case
poor and at-risk of school dropout), it does not suggest that levels of self-esteem are low for the entire group.

Global self-esteem is usually a summation of the person's
self-esteem (feelings about self) in a number of specific areas,
ranging from physical self to academic self (Ramseur, 1991).
Ramseur concluded that there are four points that should be
mentioned when referring to African-American global self-esteem: namely, (a) African-Americans have been found to have
equivalent or higher levels of self-esteem than their white counterparts; (b) African-Americans often use other African-Americans as their significant others; (c) other mechanisms may be
available to insulate African-American self-esteem (e.g., utilizing a "system blame' explanation of negative events); and (d)
African-Americans and whites may not have equivalent evaluations of various aspects of the self.

In a major review of the literature on self-esteem, Cross (1985)
found that seventy-one percent of African-Americans in the
study were found to have self-esteem levels that were equal to
or exceeded those of whites. A small percentage (sixteen percent) were found to have higher levels of self-esteem than whites,
and thirteen percent had mixed results. Essentially, this review

of over 100 self-esteem studies showed that African-Americans and whites have equivalent levels of self-esteem. This is a somewhat significant finding in that students are often placed for treatment or referred for recommended educational programs (e.g., special education) based upon studies that suggest low levels of self-concept or self-esteem being directly correlated to their socioeconomic level. In addition to some automatic assumptions about low self-esteem is the equally damaging assumption that low self-esteem is associated with drug or alcohol abuse (Moore, Laflin, and Weis, 1996). The findings in this study supported earlier research that concluded there is no relationship between low levels of self-esteem and the use of cigarettes, other types of tobacco, marijuana, alcohol, and/or other drugs.

SELF-ESTEEM AND SCHOOL INTERACTION

Weisman (1991) noted that the self-esteem movement in schools has been accompanied by the publication of hundreds of books, curricula, musical programs, and training packages, mainly designed for classroom use. The fact that self-esteem has become a predominant concern is illustrated by the fact that "30,000 copies of the California Task Force Report, *Toward A State of Esteem*, have been distributed nationwide" (p. 12). There have been a number of significant studies that have examined the role of self-esteem and school interaction. Hoge, Smit, and Hanson (1990) have indicated that there are several major variables that impact student self-esteem during the academic years. These variables include a combination of school components such as teacher interaction, the role of the principal, and the climate of the building. Additional considerations would also include family and intelligence issues. Hoge et al. (1990) identified a study by the National Center for Self-Esteem which suggested that as students get older, there was a corresponding decrease in their self-esteem. This study found that eighty-nine percent of kindergarten students reported high levels of self-esteem, only twenty percent of fifth graders, five percent of high school graduates, and only two percent of college graduates indicated they have high self-esteem.

Scott, et al. (1996) identified a study by Stipek (1984) in which the author noted:

> Children enter school expecting to be successful and feeling good about themselves and are not particularly concerned about achievement outcomes. Over time, however, they learn to care about grades and come to have negative beliefs about the likelihood of experiencing success. These changes are attributed, in part, to the manner in which children process feedback about their performance as their cognitive development continues. More important, however, they come to accept the emphasis on external evaluation for achievement that is common in school systems (p. 14).

As suggested earlier, one successful component to building self-esteem among all students is to focus on community-related issues and student involvement. The concept of a community-based interaction for students is not new. Completing community service as a technique for building self-esteem in children is worthy of consideration. Adams (1993) supports using community service programs because "the interest in community service is a way to help develop positive self-esteem and help students feel valued" (p. 53). Community service as a tool to build self-esteem assists students to learn responsibility as well as leads to becoming productive citizens. Adams also identified that the opportunity to work with adults in the community builds self-esteem.

CONTEMPORARY THEMES IN SELF-ESTEEM

There is clear support for the impact of a positive relationship between self-esteem and academic achievement (McCarty, 1997; Nichols, 1996). Most school organizations attempt to organize a program or project specifically aimed at increasing the self-esteem of low-performing students. This section on contemporary themes in self-esteem issues will look at two issues: (a) neurobiological research on self-esteem, and (b) project-focused, self-esteem initiatives.

NEUROBIOLOGICAL RESEARCH ON SELF-ESTEEM

One contemporary theme in analyzing self-esteem entails determining a relationship between self-esteem, serotonin and neurobiological research. Sylwester (1997) has suggested that recent research developments in brain chemistry may provide additional insight into self-esteem issues, impulsivity, and reckless school behavior. Sylwester indicated "recent studies with human and non-human primates suggest that fluctuations in the neurotransmitter, serotonin, plays an important role in regulating our level of self-esteem and our place within the social hierarchy" (p. 77). Simply put, the theory suggests that high levels of serotonin in the brain are associated with high self-esteem and social status. Consequently, low levels of serotonin in the brain are associated with low self-esteem and low social status. The author noted "high serotonin levels are associated with the calm assurance that leads to smoothly controlled movements, and low serotonin levels with the irritability that leads to impulsive, uncontrolled, reckless, aggressive, violent, or suicidal behavior" (p. 77).

Sylwester's theory also indicates a hierarchy in self-esteem, which supports a process that humans use to move in and out of social systems. Self-esteem is challenged when the sense of self does not match with the system's response to our own perceptions. Sylwester (1997) noted:

> It is adaptive for social species (like humans) to develop a system that arranges groups into reasonably hierarchical arrangements to perform various group tasks. The entire group benefits if survival-related tasks are assigned to those who are generally recognized to be the most capable. But things often don't work the way we'd like them to (p. 75-76).

The educational implications of Sylwester's work may be interesting for urban school leaders to review. Interaction with school leaders who provide positive social feedback "can be nature's way of regulating the serotonin system" (p. 79). As a result, creating positive feedback in the classroom can be viewed as a significant social tool to increase a student's self-esteem.

This approach correlates with other research on self-esteem which places emphasis on providing opportunities for students to increase their social stability.

PROJECT FOCUSED SELF-ESTEEM INITIATIVES

Nichols and Utesch (1998) were interested in determining whether student motivation and self-esteem would increase for students in a large urban high school, if they participated in an alternative learning program. Most of the students attending the alternative learning program had experienced a number of suspensions from their home school and were at risk of dropping out of school. While students attended the alternative learning program, they received special attention to address their specific needs through individual and group counseling periods. The general results of the study suggested that students who completed the program experienced a significant increase in self-esteem, self-efficacy, and goal orientation. Nichols and Utesch noted:

> Students who failed to complete the alternative learning program were initially significantly higher in extrinsic motivation. This suggests that dropouts may be motivated by extrinsic rewards to the point that they fail to make the connection between high school graduation and future success in the workplace. The immediate extrinsic rewards that may come from part-time jobs or other factors may circumvent the goals of continued enrollment resulting in high school graduation (p. 277).

What is significant for urban school leaders is the need to correlate future goals with activities and projects that presently need attention. When a number of the major urban centers are confronted with extremely high dropout rates, the self-esteem of students may be the only element that will keep a child coming to school.

A recent study by Cardelle-Elawar (1996) generally supports the themes expressed by Sylwester. Cardelle-Elawar's study described a teaching approach to help improve the self-esteem of Hispanic children. The primary premise of the teaching approach was to remove the stereotypes teachers had about the ability and success levels of Hispanic children. This approach originated from a metacognitive theory that had two primary objectives: (a) to develop teachers' awareness of their thinking process and (b) to establish objectives and appropriate guidance in self-assessment for students. The premise of Cardelle-Elawar's work is that teachers play a critical role in developing and maintaining self-esteem levels of at-risk, underrepresented students.

Finally, Fenzel, Magaletta, and Peyrot (1997) provided additional support specifically studying African-American adolescents and their perceptions of self-esteem with respect to the level of school strain. Their study describes the impact of school strain or sources of school-related stress. This stress is particularly significant at the middle-school level where students are challenged by peer pressure, conflicts, teacher control issues, school performance, and classroom work requirements (Munsch and Wampler, 1993). As a result of these stressors, at-risk urban students are uniquely challenged by issues of self-esteem, high-school graduation, and success in life.

The study by Fenzel, et al. (1997) examined 102 urban students who were enrolled in an academic intervention program. The study confirmed what most school leaders already suspected; that is, students reported a consistent relationship to peer strain and self-esteem as well as strain with teacher relations and school demands for scholastic competence and intrinsic motivation. This study specifically examined African-American students and found that the males experienced greater peer strain than did females. The authors concluded that "[t]he study shows that attending to the sources of strain experienced by African American middle school students in large urban middle schools is important for maintaining high levels of self-worth, school functioning, and engagement in the learning process" (p. 286).

SUMMARY

A substantial body of research indicates that African-Americans demonstrate lower self-esteem than do their white counterparts (Jensen, 1969; Pollard, 1989). Given the widespread concern regarding the achievement levels for underrepresented populations in particular, school districts are seeking ways to enhance the self-esteem and subsequently, the academic performance of these students. While the results of research that has examined self-esteem is far from conclusive, it clearly indicates a relationship exists between self-esteem and the school achievement of underrepresented students. In summary, Black (1991) has observed some of the significant aspects of the research relating to self-esteem:

♦ Most self-esteem research was conducted by psychologists and behaviorists who studied personality and the self during the 1960s and 1970s.

♦ Parents and others in the home and family have the most influence on a child's self-esteem.

♦ Schools have the power to enhance or subdue students' self-esteem through policies and practices, curriculum and instruction, institutional climate, and teacher personality and attitudes. The factors in a school that most affect student self-esteem are climate, grouping, decision-making and systems of reward and punishment.

♦ Self-esteem is usually higher among elementary school children and generally becomes more negative as students progress through the grades.

♦ Teachers can enhance self-esteem by encouraging parent involvement, involving students in classroom planning, giving students opportunities to cooperate, and trusting students to carry out learning activities responsibly.

♦ The best way for a school to have a positive effect on students' self-esteem is to foster an environment in which individuals are always respected and valued.

It should be mentioned that self-esteem in and of itself should not be a measure by which urban schools determine the overall behaviors and disposition of urban children. The literature suggests that self-esteem is an inclusive variable. In other words, the self-esteem that students display or demonstrate is a variable that includes a number of other significant components such as family, community, and interactions at school. I would suggest that self-esteem be viewed as part of the total school environment and that self-esteem issues should be included in any urban school restructuring. The effort should be on viewing the school as a community and recognizing that the self-esteem children display is critical to the success of the overall urban community. This perspective is consistent with the work of Eaton (1997). It is clear that psychosocial variables like self-esteem play a role in the comprehensive achievement of urban children.

RECOMMENDATIONS FOR PRACTICE FOR URBAN SCHOOL LEADERS

The following is a list of recommendations for urban school leaders regarding techniques and strategies to address contextual challenges for underrepresented students. Some of the recommendations also address circular hopelessness, poverty, and violence. All of the factors have a significant impact of the lives of children living in urban school communities.

- Each student should be treated as an individual and not as a group or number. Urban students experience socialization like others in American culture. As a result, the way in which these students interact with professionals in the school setting will have a significant impact on their attitudes and behaviors in the school setting.

- Efforts should be made by urban school leaders to expand the curriculum to include the contributions and cultural implications of all ethnic and racial groups. This includes an authentic appreciation by urban school leaders and not a once a week or once a month program aimed at honoring a special group. All groups should feel a part of the entire curriculum and culture of the school. Urban school leaders are responsible for ensuring that each child will feel a sense of association and belonging to the school he or she attends.

♦ Topics on race, racism, gender equity, and poverty should be a part of the continuing dialogue in the school and community. In other words, urban school leaders must continue to articulate the current issues and challenges faced by urban students. This dialogue should be collaborative in nature and collective in action. The dialogue should include community leaders, politicians, school officials (including teachers), parents, human resource organizations, and urban students.

♦ Continued research should be conducted by practitioners "in the field" who can describe daily interactions with urban students to successfully create effective programs that clearly meet the needs of children. This research should take the form of case studies, interviews, ethnographic studies, and all forms of qualitative research. These stories must become action plans for implementation and change.

♦ Special research and interest should continue on Hispanic and Native American students. Given the projected growth trend in Hispanics during the next several decades, policies, programs, and strategies that enhance their culture, values, norms, history, and family dynamics should become a part of the school curriculum and immersed into daily discussion by urban school leaders. Additionally, Native American students will require both urban school leaders and those from smaller communities to include their history and culture in curriculum as well as bring their contributions to full status consistent with contributions from other cultures.

♦ Urban school leaders in all segments of the school organizations must combat the psychological damage caused by circular hopelessness. This strategy will require the identified leaders in systemic organizations to collaborative on development and enhancement approaches for students and parents in urban settings. Leaders from the legal, financial, political, health and family, social services, and business communities must collaborate with strategies, techniques, and approaches aimed at improving urban education.

♦ Poverty must be addressed in a systematic manner involving all stakeholders in the school community. The relationship between circular hopelessness, poverty, and crime is obvious. Children need to understand their value in a culture where every aspect of your life is determined by status and position.

♦ Violence prevention programs must be established and supported by all members of the urban school community. Programs should begin in preschool and continue through the twelfth grade. Collaboration again is the key to success in this program. This requires the key leaders in the community to feel the need that this area deserves attention before it can be addressed in a positive manner.

♦ Avoid stereotyping of students and families in urban communities. This includes avoiding stereotyping Asian-American students as the model minority. All Asian students can not be expected to be genuineness in math and science and all African-American students can not be expected to be outstanding on the basketball court. Special efforts should be made by urban school leaders to distinguish behaviors between those displayed in the media (films and music videos) from the "everyday-ness" of life in urban America.

♦ It is in the interest of all Americans to respect and honor cultural heritages. This respect and honor occur in our daily interaction with children. Children are very intelligent and can quickly tell if we are either scared or intimidated by them. Let's show urban students that we are neither scared nor intimidated by them. We simply love them.

♦ Academic achievement must be a priority by all stakeholders in the urban school and community. This emphasis on academics must be stressed on a daily basis by teachers, administrators, students, parents, social service agencies, and community action groups.

♦ Monthly or bi-monthly assessment and evaluation of progress by urban students should be held in churches, activity centers, and libraries throughout the urban community. Strict requirements should be established to ensure attendance by both students and parents.

♦ Weekend and summer programs should be designed to focus on academic achievement of urban students in the classroom. These programs can be staffed by retired teachers and community activists. Students would be required to attend with a parent or guardian and school work would be completed consistent with the request of the classroom teacher.

♦ Increased technology should be made available to urban parents at accessible locations in the urban community. Students and parents would be required to attend workshops and seminars on becoming competent in computer technology and specifically in ways in which technology can enhance school performance and standards of living.

♦ Summer school should be a requirement for students who do not achieve at grade level, beginning in the first grade. While the child is attending summer school, the parent or guardian would be required to demonstrate that the child has received a minimal number of parent-child contact hours in the home.

♦ Self-esteem and personal awareness seminars should be offered by the school in collaboration with community agencies. In fact, these programs could be required for students and parents where specific problems or issues have been identified.

♦ Teacher interaction with students about self-esteem and self-worth should be encouraged. A kind word and a smile can go a long way for students.

- ♦ Specific academic programs aimed at African-American males and females should be organized and supported by urban school leaders. In addition, programs and classes for other underrepresented populations should be encouraged.

4

THE CONTEMPORARY URBAN TEACHER

INTRODUCTION

Urban teachers are the backbone of the urban school organization. Reform efforts that do not address issues affecting urban teachers will be ineffective strategies to improve the academic and social challenges of urban children. This chapter reviews the importance of urban teachers and describes the kinds of challenges they face. It also explores strategies for improving urban education. Particular emphasis is given to issues associated with preparing teachers for urban schools and more specifically the need to recruit and retain African-American teachers in regular and special-education classes. The chapter also addresses future considerations and some summary perspectives.

THE IMPORTANCE OF TEACHERS AND CHALLENGES TO THE PROFESSION

Most professionals become educators because they love teaching and they also love children. There is something special about the nature of the relationship between a student who enjoys learning and a teacher who enjoys teaching. Often, young teachers express idealistic feelings about teaching, while veteran teachers are more mature and guided in their idealism.

Parkay and Hardcastle-Stanford (1995) described the most popular reasons people are attracted to teaching. The reasons included the love of (a) teaching, (b) students, (c) subject matter, (d) teaching life and social skills, and (e) the teaching-learning process. The authors also suggest that teachers have tremendous influence, particularly noticeable in the early elementary years. This is a time when teachers tend to be revered and respected by their young students.

Most teachers decide to become teachers before they go to college (Parkay and Hardcastle-Stanford, 1995). These teachers cite that early in their careers they find teaching rewarding and meaningful. Dr. Karen Patterson-Stewart, formerly a professor at Kent State University and now president and chief executive officer of Patterson-Stewart Consulting Services, suggests that teaching is an art that requires risk-taking and an emphasis on affective learning. She suggests that in order to achieve outstanding instructional interaction, teachers must believe in what they are teaching and saying in addition to developing the cognitive understanding of the content area. We can remember special teachers who inspired us to enter the field of education. While many of us joke about our love of teaching, our commitment to the field of education, our hours and vacations, the reality is that most educators teach simply because they like it.

There is no question that the teachers who continuously indicate they love teaching will continue to inspire and motivate students. However, the growing tide of behaviors and attitudes expressed by teachers suggest serious impediments exist in the effort to attract quality candidates into the teaching field. Because of the unique challenges associated with urban teaching, there is an even greater struggle to recruit and retain effective urban teachers. Some of the challenges facing teachers in general include classroom-management concerns, violence, drug-abuse issues, increasing levels of paperwork, securing and maintaining parental support, and long working hours. Other challenges noted by Johnson, Collins, Dupius, and Johansen (1995) include the lack of proper financial support, difficulty in getting good teachers, diminishing moral standards, problems with administration, too much emphasis on sports, teachers' strikes, and a general lack of respect for teachers. The scope of this chapter will identify and discuss some of the significant aspects for teachers in urban schools; (a) issues associated with preparing teachers for urban schools, and (b) a special focus on the need for African-American teachers. The chapter concludes with some future considerations for urban teachers.

PREPARING TEACHERS FOR URBAN SCHOOLS

In 1969, William Perel and Philip Vairo indicated the need to recruit and prepare teachers for urban schools as one of the greatest challenges facing big-city schools. Most of Perel and Vairo's focus was directed toward teacher-preparation programs. They proposed that preservice teachers be trained in effective techniques for meaningful interaction with children from urban environments. One of the more common strategies implemented by most teacher-education programs at universities is the field experience. In most cases, the students are exposed to field experience in order to introduce them to varieties of school organizations. Most colleges make an attempt to introduce preservice teachers to urban schools. Unfortunately, as Jackson May (1997) indicated, these field experiences tend to confirm stereotypes that the many white female preservice teachers held prior to their field experience. In other words, when preservice teachers complete their field experiences in urban settings, the experience confirms stereotypes more solidly.

Perel and Vairo (1969) suggested nearly twenty-eight years ago that professors tended to demonstrate little interest in teacher-training for teachers who would practice in inner-city schools. In fact, the professors themselves try to avoid any involvement with inner-city schools. Mimi Warshaw, professor of education at California State University Dominguez Hills, described her experience when she went from the "ivory tower" of the university into an urban school in Los Angeles (1986). While her story is a humorous account of her experiences at the university versus her experiences in an urban school, she notes that today's schools function differently than the public schools with which most professors were familiar.

In addition to the preparation aspects of teacher-education, a review of the research regarding teachers that are in the classroom today clearly suggests that the changing demographics make it necessary to address issues of multiculturalism in American classrooms (Banks, 1994; Nieto, 1992; Tatum, 1992). Olmedo (1997) indicated that according to the NEA, the current demographics show that eighty-seven percent of teachers are white, eight percent are African-American, and three percent Hispanic. Two percent represent a combination of racial groups. These figures are directly opposite from the projection of the racial dynamics of students who currently attend public schools and those that will attend in the next century. For example, according to Parkay and Hardcastle-Stanford (1995), by the year 2050, African-Americans will constitute sixteen percent of the population, Hispanic-Americans will make up twenty percent, Asian-Americans will constitute eleven percent, and Anglo-European-Americans will make up fifty-three percent. Currently, however, in many urban school districts, an overwhelming majority of the students are African-American or Hispanic. In the suburban schools across the nation, however, Anglo-European-American children still constitute the majority of students. As an additional example, Olmedo (1997) cited a study which suggests that currently students of color form the majority in twenty-five of the largest school districts in the United States, and by 2010, students of color will be the largest percentage of students in over fifty major cities.

Researchers such as Martha Montero-Sieburth (1989) describe challenges urban teachers face and recommend that in order to prepare teachers for urban schools, their successes will be based on the teachers' knowledge. She noted:

> Unlike urban schools of 50 years ago, today's urban schools are a new phenomenon due to the economic, social, and demographic shifts in the functions of cities. Today's cities are multi-functional; that is, they are associated with more than one major economic activity. Urban areas are also in varying stages of development. Corridors of new construction and gentrified older neighborhoods adjoin areas of deteriorating and abandoned housing. Additionally, modern cities are characterized by cultural heterogeneity. Different ways

of life, values, and beliefs conflict or mesh as various races and ethnicity's seek respite within the boundaries of America's urban communities (p. 333).

In essence, because the schools and the communities have changed, the way in which urban teachers are prepared for the classroom also need to change. Montero-Sieburth suggested that urban teachers face changes in the comprehensive urban community such as the following:

♦ Large numbers of immigrants and students with limited English proficiency

♦ English-as-a-second-language programs

♦ Students with low socioeconomic backgrounds

♦ Social and family challenges

♦ Issues of self-esteem and identity

Teachers in urban schools must understand the reality that Montero-Sieburth noted students face: "For them [underrepresented students in urban schools], learning how to make it in America is contingent upon their passage through urban schools which represent the funnel through which they are filtered into regular mainstream classes" (p. 335). Another significant point Montero-Sieburth made pertains to the lack of control these underrepresented students and families feel in their lives outside the classroom. These feelings and this reality is of great importance to the successes teachers will achieve in their classrooms.

It is obvious that we need successful teachers in urban schools. Failure to provide adequate instructional support for urban students will lead to unacceptable failure. Peterson, Bennet, and Sherman (1991) studied common behaviors exhibited by teachers who worked successfully with at-risk students. The successful techniques in common include: (a) creation of a place of belonging and identity, (b) an identifiable academic program, (c) explicit coaching strategies for students, (d) demands and expectations placed on students, (e) quick responses to and resolution of students' problems, (f) goal-setting themes in the classroom, (g) prior teacher vision, experience, and training, and (h) small classes. The teachers in this study also noted other successful aspects of their work with at-risk students, such as parental contact, positive relationships with administrators, use of computers, and the presence of teachers whose ethnicity reflected the ethnicity of students.

The ethnicity of the teacher and the ability of the teacher to interact successfully with urban students has been recently debated in academic circles. The debate essentially centers on whether teachers who represent a traditionally underrepresented group can be more effective with students of similar backgrounds than teachers who represent the majority culture. The study by Peterson, Bennet, and Sherman (1991) indicated that some teachers successfully used their own ethnicity to interact with students. There were teachers from other cultures as well who were successful with traditionally underrepresented students. The authors noted "successful teachers make their impact in a variety of areas of students' needs, and they work with a variety of approaches and personal strengths" (p. 186). It appears that school boards and other stakeholders in urban schools should support individuals who demonstrate an interest in working with urban students, regardless of the ethnicity of the teacher. However, there must be a serious, concerted effort to attract more underrepresented teachers into education and specifically those teachers who want to work in urban schools. There are no schools in greater need of identifying teachers from underrepresented backgrounds than urban schools.

SPECIAL FOCUS ON RECRUITING AND RETAINING AFRICAN-AMERICAN TEACHERS

All educational and social institutions face the demand of recruiting and retaining outstanding personnel in their organizations. It has been documented in the literature that there is a shortage of teachers of color in public education (Goodlad, 1990) and urban schools in particular (Irvine, 1990; Jones and Sandidge, 1997). Colleges of education frequently receive requests from school districts about the availability of minority preservice teachers scheduled to graduate. Some districts offer contracts to

THE CONTEMPORARY URBAN TEACHER

underrepresented education majors during their junior year of college in an effort to recruit teachers of color. The opportunity for African-American students to interact with African-American teachers and administrators should not be understated. All students in urban schools need to observe and interact with African-Americans and other traditionally underrepresented professionals on a daily basis.

Jones and Sandidge (1997) noted that for various reasons new and returning teachers do not seek out urban schools as their preferred environment. The authors cite a study by Feistrizer (1990) which indicated "a survey of 3,201 teachers hired since 1985 indicates that only 12% of these teachers would be willing to teach in urban schools, even in the face of a severe teacher shortage" (p. 193). Jones and Sandidge (1997) also reported that a small number of undergraduate students (approximately 18 percent) indicated that they would consider an urban school environment. Schwartz (1996) adds "fuel to the flame" by indicating that in urban districts like New York City, teachers who are entering the profession do not plan to stay a significant time in urban schools. A significant number of teachers who currently teach in urban schools express a desire to be employed some place else. Schwartz reports that one of every three teachers in New York City leaves after three years. The reasons expressed by teachers for leaving urban schools include issues of safety, curriculum concerns, ineffective bureaucracy, low parental involvement, and funding concerns (King, 1993). Needless to say, the reasons stated by teachers who do not want to teach in urban schools and those who are there but looking to get out suggests there is a need to examine reasons associated with the absence of the African-American teacher in urban schools.

THE ABSENCE OF AFRICAN-AMERICAN TEACHERS

Urban parents often ask their boards of education: "Why aren't there more African-American teachers hired in this district?" Superintendents and school boards typically respond that there is a dwindling pool of African-American teacher candidates and that there is fierce competitiveness associated with recruiting and retaining African-American teachers. Suburban districts are also interested in hiring African-American teachers for their districts so that they can address diversity initiatives in their communities. There is general consensus among scholars that the African-American teaching population will continue to diminish and that African-American educators will likely represent less than five percent of all teachers within the next five years.

In order to understand comprehensively the current status of African-American teachers, we need to understand the historical context of this issue. Irvine (1990) stated that historically teaching was one of the few professions accessible to African-Americans and as a result, teaching was perceived to be a position of high social status within the African-American community. Irvine suggests that the teaching profession was particularly attractive for African-American females. Essentially, teaching, nursing, and social work were the careers in which African-American females were readily accepted.

It is clear that there was one significant social event that had a tremendous impact on the quantity of African-American teachers and their availability to teach in urban communities. The *Brown* decision served as a major turning point for African-American teachers, because it essentially changed the order of decision-making for boards of education. Prior to *Brown*, any decisions regarding the African-American schools were determined by African-American administrators. After *Brown*, personnel decisions by European-American administrators resulted in a number of African-American teachers being fired or reassigned to schools in all-white communities. Ethridge (cited in Irvine, 1990) estimated that between 1954 and 1972 there were at least 39,386 documented cases of African-American teachers who lost their jobs in seventeen southern states. Consequently, the number of African-American teachers has been declining for the last forty-three years. There appears to be little that can stop this trend (Irvine, 1990).

The shortage of African-American male teachers must be addressed. The literature has sufficiently addressed the absence of African-American male teachers; however, it is equally important to discuss the two primary roles of the African-American male teachers: to add to the gender diversity in the school environment, and to serve as role models and father figures for both African-American males and females. The presence of African-American males in elementary and secondary public urban schools is an important component for districts to consider.

SIGNIFICANT FACTORS CONTRIBUTING TO THE DECLINE IN THE NUMBER OF AFRICAN-AMERICAN TEACHERS

African-American students currently make up approximately sixteen percent of the students in public schools nationwide. Irvine (1988) discusses four major reasons regarding the decline in numbers of African-American teachers:

- The decline in the number of teacher-education majors overall
- The decline in African-American college students in general
- Widening career options for African-Americans
- The institutionalization of the teacher competency tests

Irvine refers to studies by Baratz and Zwerling who noted:

College attendance rates among blacks in general are plummeting. Although blacks comprise 13% of 18-24 year-olds, they represent only 9% of students enrolled in college. In 1977, one-half of all black high school graduates enrolled in college. This number fell to 36% by 1982. When black students do attend college, 42% of them attend 2 year colleges, where approximately 75% of those entering leave and never return. Fewer than 12% complete a 4-year degree; fewer than 5% attend graduate or professional schools (p. 505).

The decline in teacher-education majors from underrepresented populations and the declining enrollment of African-American college students are issues directly associated with

the K–12 experience. Irvine noted that these discouraging numbers are a result of tracking in high school "where students are
disproportionately assigned to low-level, non-college-prepara-
tory curricula; increased graduation and college entrance requirements; negative teacher expectations; and the growing number
of black children from female-headed households" (p. 504).

It should be noted here that a female-headed household is
not an absolute indicator for school failure. There is a tendency,
however, for school officials to assume a child from a one-par-
ent family is emotionally and psychologically dysfunctional. This
is not the case and administrators, counselors, and teachers
should be aware of this issue. Studies of single-parent households that are led primarily by females do suggest, however, an
ever-shifting role in the traditional nuclear family and in most
cases suggest that the one parent is completing tasks and responsibilities normally completed by two parents.

A continuing trend on college campuses is the obvious low
number of African-Americans in teacher education programs
and the notion that education is perceived as a low status occupation. This has been a major shift from the historical context
within the African-American community when teaching and
education were perceived to be important occupations within
the community. Irvine noted that for African-American females
in particular, there has been a shift in occupations typically re-
served only for females. In other words, Irvine suggested that
"these factors are no longer very relevant for a generation that
is less likely to relegate women to certain occupations, a generation that is more likely to delay marriage and childbearing, and
more likely to have dual-career marriages in which men play a
significant parenting role" (p. 505). As a result, it is increasingly
difficult to recruit and retain African-American teachers, especially those who desire to teach in urban settings.

The impact of the institutionalization of teacher competency
tests has also had an impact on African-American teacher candidates. According to results indicated by Irvine, there is a national trend for African-American teacher candidates to lag
behind their majority counterparts. As with most standardized
test, there is a need to examine issues related to "cultural bias,
lack of content and predictive validity, and inability to measure

crucial affective qualities such as dedication, motivation, and caring" (p. 506).

A Focus on Special Education and African-Americans

The disproportionate placement of African-Americans in special education programs deserves a great deal of attention and investigation. Russo and Talbert-Johnson (1997) provide an excellent overview of the overrepresentation of African-Americans in special-education programs and offer some background information and reasons for this concern.

In special-education programs, the percentage of African-American students is often twice their percentage in the general student population. The data that Russo and Talbert-Johnson provide should be very disturbing to educators. The authors refer to a study by Jennings (1994), which indicates that according to the 1990 census, 31.9 percent of African-Americans live below the poverty line. Accordingly, "this statistic is further exacerbated relative to special education in light of related data that more than 57% of all African-Americans who live below the poverty level reside in urban areas" (p. 140).

According to the Council for Exceptional Children (1994), African-Americans make up approximately twenty-eight percent of all students in special education, although African-Americans constitute only sixteen percent of the overall population. Russo and Talbert-Johnson suggest the range for African-American involvement in this program should be between 14.4 percent and 17.6 percent. This question becomes obvious: Why is there an overrepresentation of African-American students in special education? One explanation is rooted in test bias. Russo and Talbert-Johnson cite the first major court case pertaining to African-Americans and special education. The case involved African-American student, Larry P. Riles and occurred in San Francisco. It dealt with an overrepresentation of African-Americans in EMR (educable mentally retarded) classes. In the Riles case, African-Americans represented 28.5 percent of the student population, but represented 66 percent of the students in EMR. In the final analysis, Russo and Talbert-Johnson stated "the appellate court, in affirming earlier judgments, not only agreed that the San Francisco Unified School District violated the rights of students by relying on nonvalidated intelligence (IQ) tests, but also ordered the state to develop plans to eliminate the disproportionate enrollment of African American children in classes for the EMR" (p. 139). Although this case was seen as favorable toward the African-American students, similar cases with similar evidence have resulted in rulings against African-American students.

Some of the recommendations for changing the overrepresentation by African-Americans in special education classes include restructuring teacher-education programs, preparing teachers to become culturally responsive, increasing efforts to recruit teachers of color, recognizing and valuing individuals, using assessment instruments for guiding instruction, determining best practices for improved student learning, and developing home-school-community partnerships (Russo and Talbert-Johnson, 1997).

FUTURE CONSIDERATIONS FOR URBAN TEACHERS

African-American teachers in urban schools are significant and important to the school organization as well as to the children they serve. One of the reasons these educators are important to children is that they serve as role models. Cole (1986) suggested that as role models, African-American teachers are able to influence the behaviors and actions of urban children and are instrumental in directing them to positive actions within the school context. While having role models is important for urban youth in terms of self-identity and self-esteem, there are other organizational issues that urban teachers must consider for the future. These issues include, but are not limited to, funding initiatives and issues of safety and violence.

School funding for urban schools is currently debated across the country. President Clinton recently announced a major, multimillion dollar grant for urban school initiatives. A major amount of the money is slated to fund teacher and staff development and professional renewal initiatives. Unequal spending on urban education is not a new concern or issue for urban educators. In the early 1970s, there were court cases such as *Serrano v. Priest* in which the California Supreme Court ruled the state's system of school finance was unconstitutional based on the Fourteenth Amendment and California's equal protection policies. Other funding concerns focus on building repair needs and financial resources for computer and related technology upgrades.

URBAN TEACHERS AND TECHNOLOGY

One of the fastest growing areas of inequity for urban teachers and children is in access to technology and related computer applications. Because of the obvious financial expense of computers, urban schools are unlikely to have computer programs commensurate with suburban schools. As a result, urban children are likely to be the biggest losers in educational technology. We are living in a computer-dependent society and job potential and the ability to maintain basic living arrangements will require solid computer skills. The failure of urban children to be exposed to this technology will be one of the major challenges in the twenty-first century. Bill Moyer's documentary on school funding provided examples of technological discrepancies that exist between urban and suburban schools (Moyer, 1996).

URBAN TEACHERS AND SAFETY ISSUES

Another major consideration for urban teachers in the twenty-first century will be attention to safety in urban schools. It is important to mention that violence and safety concerns are expressed by teachers from all geographical settings. In fact, there have been several reports that indicated that violence is increasing in rural and suburban areas at rates that surprise many individuals. Jones and Sandidge (1997) cited studies by Hechinger (1994) and Kingery, Mirzaee, Pruitt, and Hurley (1990) that suggested that violence is increasing in rural and suburban schools. While most teachers do not have to be concerned about being assaulted and experiencing violence, preservice teachers and the general public maintain the view that urban schools are to be feared and vacated as soon as possible. A common practice in urban schools for many years has been that inexperienced teachers are assigned to low-achieving and high-poverty schools. Teachers with seniority and tenure tend to select schools that have less poverty and more higher achieving students. In urban environments, teachers who transfer from high-poverty and low-achieving schools with a substantial percentage of underrepresented students typically encounter less diversity after reassignment to higher achieving schools.

Jones and Sandidge (1997) provide several excellent approaches to dealing with school violence:

♦ Create smaller classes

♦ Treat students as individuals

♦ Create welcoming and supportive environments

♦ Involve parents in schools

♦ Emphasize relationships instead of rules

♦ Incorporate conflict resolution strategies into curriculum

♦ Involve students in peer mediation of conflicts

♦ Add parents as part of school programming

SUCCESSFUL TEACHING

Illmer, Snyder, Erbaugh, and Kurz (1997) provide a contemporary analysis of urban teachers' perceptions about successful teaching. In the 1997 study, Illmer et al. analyzed interviews with seventy-three educators (forty-five teachers, eighteen student teachers, and ten teacher-educators) in Detroit City Schools. The results of the study yielded forty-five themes from the group who were asked eight interview questions. The seven themes (issues) that received the highest rank were (a) knowledge of the community and culture, (b) teachers' needs and attitudes, (c) children's needs, (d) instructional style and teaching methodology, (e) community resources, (f) school climate, and (g) subject matter and content knowledge. The primary results of the study suggested "early teacher preparation experiences should incorporate opportunities for preservice teachers to recognize the importance of learning about the communities in which they will work and the cultures of the students they will teach" (p. 383). The second major finding supported closer working relationships between experienced and preservice teachers. Linda Darling-Hammond (1995) has indicated that issues such as inequality and access to knowledge are imporant for teachers to consider when interacting with urban youth. Teachers are concerned about organizational and relational issues and about physical building, or facilities.

Of all of the recommendations previously listed, the ideas that can be implemented immediately are those that require teachers and urban professionals to transform their belief systems for the benefit of children. While treating students as individuals and creating welcoming environments may seem easy, these activities genuinely require professionals to make a long-term commitment to working with children who are poor and disenfranchised. This type of commitment involves more than what we receive from the motivational speaker who often kicks off a school year. It is an attitude to be exhibited throughout the school year. Resources should be made available for these motivational and workshop speakers to work with students and urban professionals throughout the year.

SUMMARY PERSPECTIVES FOR URBAN TEACHERS

George McKenna (1988) talked about the need to secure African-American teachers for the classroom. He provided interesting data that symbolizes the severity of the demand. He noted in 1988 that Michigan only had eleven African-American male teachers below the age of twenty-seven. He also noted that in California during this same period, fewer that one-hundred African-American students were enrolled in undergraduate teaching programs in the state's five largest universities. Needless to say, these are problems that need serious attention with respect to urban teachers. McKenna's perspective regarding the issue of who should teach in urban schools is compelling. McKenna stated, "The quality of a teacher, that is, his or her ability to effectively educate children, has nothing to do with the ethnicity of the teacher. Excellence is not limited to any particular group, nor is it excluded from any" (p. 121).

McKenna believes that the best teachers should have three qualities: (a) knowledge of their subject matter, (b) a nurturing and serving attitude toward students, and (c) an understanding of the learning process. A good teacher is a person who exemplifies these qualities and possesses a vision for the big picture of schooling. Schools should not be forced to be evaluated on the basis of one day or one week; teachers must look at schools from the standpoint of where they would like to see their students in the very near future.

One of the interesting proposals Jones and Sandidge (1997) supported was the creation of innovative ways to recruit individuals into urban education. They recommended alternative routes to education certification. In addition to the university-based teacher-education program, these authors suggested creating ways for non-traditional students to enter the field of education. Such programs exist in a number of cities including Sandusky, Ohio, where the superintendent and board of education, interested in hiring more minority candidates, created a program to pay for coursework at the local university branch in an effort to secure more minority teachers. The program was co-sponsored by a local business and grants from the state department of education. The early results of the program have been promising.

Teachers in urban schools also need support from administrators, superintendents, school boards, and parents. The successful urban schools will be those able to bring these parties together for the benefit of urban children. Teachers need economic incentive and appreciation from a culture and community that owe them a debt of gratitude. They also need the following advantages:

- Decreased class size
- Classroom teacher aides
- Additional resources such as computers and modern equipment
- Professional development training

Decreased class size has been proven to create a more positive relationship between the teacher and student and to lead to enhanced academic productivity from the student. Decreased class size usually requires more money for additional teachers. In a time when urban districts are struggling to get levies approved by the public, this is a difficult request. However, when urban education begins to invest in teacher education issues such as smaller classes and more teacher aides, we will begin to see results from the classroom teachers. At the same time, as teachers are provided with these resources, they must be held accountable for the achievement of specific goals and objectives related to the success of their students.

The need for additional resources for computers was addressed earlier in this chapter, but the necessity is immediate and long-term: students need to start learning on and about state-of-the-art computers today and continue to learn on updated equipment. The final component of professional development training is crucial for teacher success. Revenue must be provided for teachers to remain current and updated in their curriculum and disciplines. Teachers should also have the opportunity to interact with other teachers from their own district and from other parts of the country in order to share ideas and be successful.

Pipho (1995) provides a summary of another consideration urban teachers will likely address very soon: the issue of privatization, charter schools, and vouchers. Most of these proposals are presented because the perception is that our schools—especially our urban schools—are out of control and are functioning in an unacceptable manner. There can be no urban school reform without teachers playing a vital role. Teacher unions and boards of education should ask two questions at the beginning and end of every meeting: What will we do at this meeting to help urban kids? What did we do at this meeting to help urban kids?

Other contemporary approaches to urban restructuring involving teachers include the effort to reorganize or decentralize urban schools. This effort is noteworthy and significant. This approach works in much the same way as making the individual classroom smaller for efficiency and increased productivity. Even districts such as Los Angeles with 640,000 students see the merit in making the district smaller and more accountable. Decentralization diminishes the traditional role of the central office and puts fiscal management responsibilities at the level where decisions should be made. These community-based schools should have four primary objectives: increasing achievement, increasing attendance and improving behavior, reducing violence and related harm to students and faculty, and increasing the input and involvement of parents in the decision-making process.

Lee Morganet (1991) has made a worthy recommendation. He focuses on the importance of building strong and effective relationships with students. The supposition is that these relationships will be helpful in both motivating students and decreasing discipline problems. Sometimes the insight into the resolution of complex problems can be found in the nature of the relationship between the two central parties. In urban schools, the two central parties are the student and the teacher. The importance of caring about students as individuals and collectively will provide opportunities for good will between students and teachers. Critical factors such as communication and how messages are communicated are important in building relationships. Morganet suggests that "people tend to be attracted to others who seem interested in them and like them. It is reaffirming to be accepted and valued" (p. 260). If teachers talked and listened to students, it would cost very little and would add little to the district's budget. Successful urban teachers have rules, are tough, fair, and have excellent communication skills with students.

I do not want to suggest that teaching in an urban school in the twenty-first century will be easy. I do believe, however, that the answer and central theme to rebuilding urban schools is found in building community. The urban school must become a community where students, teachers, parents and administrators share ideas, values, and beliefs. This community includes all stakeholders and it begins with the teacher who stands in the front of the class.

5

THE URBAN PRINCIPAL

INTRODUCTION

Research on the school principalship has consistently concluded that the principal is a central figure in the school organization. School principalship is viewed as significant in terms of initiating change at the building level. The principal sets the tone and influences the climate of the building. The scope and nature of the urban principal's role in any aspect of school reform or restructuring are strongly influenced by the socioeconomic and institutional environment within which the school exists. The conditions in which urban principals work are often challenging and require an additional commitment often to achieve marginal success. Successful urban principals tend to be aware of cultural traditions, mores, and values within the community they serve. This chapter examines the role of the urban principal in a number of ways. The principal is in a powerful and influential position in the school community, which requires the principal to incorporate a number of plans and programs into the urban school. This chapter also reviews principalship reform in urban education and offers a look at successful approaches available to the modern urban school principal. Because achievement is a major concern to all principals, and particularly to urban principals, a section of this chapter is devoted to examining curriculum and instructional aspects of this challenging administrative position. The need to investigate effective strategies to attract women and minorities into the urban principalship is also examined. The chapter concludes, specifically focusing on what the urban principals needs to accomplish to enhance community awareness and student success.

THE POWER OF THE PRINCIPALSHIP

Considerable research validates the importance of the principal's role in terms of school achievement and the far-ranging nature of their influence with faculty, staff, and students (Bossert, Dwyer, Rowan, and Lee, 1982; Crow and Glascock, 1995; Edmonds, 1979; Hallinger and Murphy, 1987; Hipp and Bredeson, 1995; Kirby and Colbert, 1994; Lomotey, 1989; Raisch and Rogus, 1995). The leadership skills and interaction of the principal with the school and community become critical elements that point to success for the entire school district. Indeed, the principal has the power to influence the culture and climate of the entire school. Although James Coleman's (1966) early research did not "paint a pretty picture" of the role of the principal and the effectiveness of education in general. Much of the contemporary research suggests that the principal is one of the key figures in school success. Bossert et al. (1982) have indicated that successful schools work primarily because there are successful principals who have at least four basic characteristics, which include (a) an ability to create a school climate that is conducive to learning and free of disciplinary problems and vandalism, (b) an emphasis on basic skills instruction schoolwide, (c) an expectation among teachers that all students can achieve, and (d) a vision to convey a system of clear instructional objectives for monitoring and assessing students' performance. Additionally, Bossert et al. stated "Moreover, the studies indicate that the principals in these successful schools are perceived to be strong programmatic leaders who know the learning problems in their classrooms and allocate resources effectively" (p. 35).

The key question for the principal becomes how can these systemic changes be made in school settings where the principal can be a strong leader and at the same time have influence over other structured, bureaucratic aspects of the school organization. The principal's role as facilitator is acutely tested in these interactions with other school personnel.

The purpose of this chapter is to explore the overall reform efforts regarding the principal's role in school and to specifically examine the urban principalship and the unique issues associated with this leadership role. Therefore, the organization of this chapter focuses on three aspects of the urban principalship: (a) principalship reform, (b) curriculum and instructional aspects of the urban principalship, and (c) the recruiting of women and minorities to the urban principalship.

PRINCIPALSHIP REFORM

As with most of the contemporary issues in school reform, principalship reform can easily be traced back to the massive educational reform movement of the early 1980s. One of the areas that has consistently been designated as an area of focus for review and restructuring has been in leadership development in school organizations. One of the early pioneers in this reform movement was Wilbur Brookover. His approach, as well as that of Ron Edmonds, suggests that any true reform in schools involves leadership and specifically leadership at the building level. Carlin (1992) noted "Reformed education requires principals with vision who have the opportunity to communicate and infuse it" (p. 46). The issue of vision is uniquely significant for principals, and other key leaders in school organizations, as many of the criticisms regarding principals are specifically focused on their lack of vision or direction for the school. As a result, the reform movement has impacted principalship in terms of leadership development and vision, unlike any other single position in the school organization excluding the chief executive officer. In fact, in many small communities the high school principal is one of the most significant and influential individuals in the community.

Edmonds (1980) identified the basic tenets of reform for students of school leadership. Successful, effective schools have the following:

- ♦ strong administrative leadership
- ♦ a sense of mission

- ◆ clear instructional focus
- ◆ high expectations of students and staff
- ◆ regular use of student achievement data for remediation
- ◆ a safe, orderly climate
- ◆ parent/community involvement

This list is not necessarily in order of priority. It is likely, however, that in order to have a truly effective school, all of these elements must play important roles. The point that is worthy of additional comment, is the notion that leadership (especially at the building level) is likely the most important aspect of the comprehensive approach to reform. Essentially, it takes a strong principal to effectively coordinate all elements of an effective school and to facilitate the overall responsibilities of the team. Carlin (1992) noted "The role of the principal receives special attention because it offers the single most immediate route to school reform. If the role can change, if it can be strengthened and its incumbent held accountable, what marvels may be worked in the improvement of each school building" (p. 26).

One consistent theme to be taken seriously by principals from both urban and non-urban environments is the focus on accountability and standards. Urban principals, more than ever, are being held accountable for the direct successes of their students and faculty. These accountability standards require that the principal build a team with the faculty and staff as well as delegate leadership within the building.

Maeroff (1993) reminds us that "a principal who undergoes team building along with teachers is more likely to end up sharing their conviction" (p. 26). In other words, not only does the principal need to focus on team-building, but he or she must become part of the team. Principals can no longer afford to send faculty away to learn new techniques or technologies at a workshop or conference; the principal must attend also. In order for the principal to be a team builder, there must be a commitment to change and reform the traditional role of the principal. "When a principal is insecure or caught up in defending the top-down hierarchy, the team's effectiveness is likely to be impaired"

(p. 26). This role change for the urban principal is particularly significant because of the need to address a number of issues at the same time. One of the problems or challenges of team-building is that principals can be reluctant to participate in team building training. In true reform mode, the principal will re-examine traditional and positional power normally associated with his or her role. It should be noted, however, that a principal can really become powerful by relinquishing power to the individuals who work for and with them. This notion is grounded in the leadership theory that true power is obtained when the leader essentially distributes power to those in the organization. This approach requires that leaders have a strong understanding of their role and mission. This approach is the essence of team-building.

Another roadblock to team-building for principals is related to the outside training and what happens when both the principal and staff return to the home school. A principal may perform satisfactorily in public—especially in public training sessions—but either disregard or minimize the importance of team-building upon return to school. This reversion potential is why urban school reform efforts must have the support of both the superintendent and board of education prior to any systematic effort to reform a school district. High-level approval of programs and procedures will send the necessary message that urban school reform is a serious matter and appropriate goals, procedures, and evaluation should be maintained.

The advantages of team-building for urban principals are clear. Teachers and principals become allies when there is consistent communication about the vision, mission, and direction of the building. Perhaps the most significant advantage of team building for the urban principal is the attention placed on student and parent involvement and ultimately student achievement. Team building permits the kind of inclusion that allows each individual to make a contribution to the team effort and more importantly, no one person has to carry the entire project alone.

Successful urban principals delegate leadership and responsibility. Delegation can be difficult in light of the sometimes stressful and anxiety-inducing interactions with unions and administrative procedures. Delegation requires the principal to develop partnerships in the building. These partnerships should be established based on what is in the best interest of children and not on union policy for teachers or principals. The nature of these partnerships should include internal faculty and staff and include individuals in the school system and board of education. Partnerships should be forged with members of the community at large as well.

Two critical elements in effective delegation of leadership and authority are the planning and communication techniques and financial resource allocation. Briefly, the urban principal must make time to effectively plan team-building activities and programming as well as effectively communicate the direction of the school to internal and external publics. The financial component suggests that budgeted money should be devoted to team-building efforts in urban schools. Messages become clear to teachers, principals, parents, and students: if there are little or no funds devoted to these reform activities, it is apparent that the identified issue is of little importance.

If we look at urban school reform from a leadership perspective, Bolman and Deal (1994) have provided some excellent guidelines for urban leaders to consider regarding leadership within the urban context. They suggested the following recommendations:

- *Leadership is learned mainly from experience.* Bolman and Deal suggest that "developing leaders involves structuring careers so that emerging novices have ample opportunities to learn from the rough and tumble, give and take, of working in organizations" (p. 87). This notion is appropriate for urban school principals. One of the current dilemmas that urban school superintendents consistently share is the need to identify and recruit quality candidates into the administrative field. Bolman and Deal also indicate that leaders can learn about organizations just as effectively by second-hand experiences.

- *Reflections and having dialogue with other professionals will also assist people in the learning process.* The need to focus on "getting feedback, reflecting on events, and entertaining new paradigms can be informal activity or a more systematic group enterprise. But lessons of leadership are also transmitted through lore, ideas, and stories in informal conversation with others" (p. 90). Retreats and faculty meetings addressing these issues are just as important as focus on tasks. They can be encouraging and supportive for principals and teachers who do not receive much reinforcement from the system, community, and parents.

♦ *Leadership can be learned by identifying and emulating exemplary leaders.* Successful urban principals work all over the country. They are extremely committed, dedicated, organized, focused on the future, and are willing to make decisions that are in the best interest of urban children. Determining what is the best approach given the context of urban schools is central to this issue.

♦ *Leadership can be taught—but not the way we currently teach it.* Bolman and Deal support a common belief in the urban community that real reform will require leaders to observe a different approach than traditional leadership. In other words, urban leaders will need to focus more on internal analysis, or "getting prospective leaders, for example, to know themselves, their strengths, limitations, and inner feelings" (p. 92). In urban schools, this internal reflection and examination of why we are doing what we do is critical to urban school reform.

Terry Deal and Kent Peterson (1991) described five major foci of school reform for urban principals that are worthy of mentioning:

♦ A focus on specific skills and needs of individuals involved in education

♦ A focus the structure and operation of the school

♦ A focus on the political realities among the constituencies within the school

♦ A focus on educational economies involving choice and related markets

♦ A focus on school culture.

Fredericks (1992) summarized some of the major challenges urban school principals face, which include (a) effectively dealing with issues of reform and restructuring through a process of group development and consensus, (b) meeting the social and educational needs of students, (c) implementing meaningful systems of staff development and empowerment, (d) facilitating the identification and implementation of meaningful school goals, and (e) evaluating progress to make appropriate midcourse adjustments. While all of these components are significant, two deserve special attention, because they epitomize urban education reform. The focus on restructuring based on the social and educational needs of students is central to any meaningful change in urban educational organizations. Attention must be directed toward a collaborative means of restructuring schools in order be able to achieve curriculum and related instructional goals. It is useless to restructure and reorganize schools, if insufficient attention is directed toward the needs of children who attend urban schools. Any solution to urban school issues must be focused on the transformation of the organization and the people within the organization.

Other aspects of urban principalship reform can be found in the research of organizations such as the national elementary and secondary principals' associations and the University Council for Educational Administration. Suggestions for reform in the principalship and other areas of school leadership have also come from business-leaders, legislators, and various accrediting agencies. Fredericks (1992) summarized the four basic assumptions that underlie reform issues for urban principals:

♦ Restructuring must be viewed as a collaborative process

♦ Restructuring and development are continuous processes that will never be finished

♦ Restructuring and development contain aspects of
assessment, goal-setting, program implementation,
and evaluation

♦ Restructuring includes meeting the general goal of
reform as well as the specific goals of changing individuals, principals, and schools.

Miller (1992) has suggested that there are encouraging signs
in urban school reform, such as finance equity law suits and
issues of professional assessment for school leaders.

While the debate continues about the direction and promise
for urban principalship reform, it is clear that all solutions involve collaboration and trust. Collaboration must exist between
stakeholders and there must be sufficient trust so that programs,
policies, and procedures can be established with the central
purpose of helping urban children grow and develop.

CURRICULUM AND INSTRUCTION ASPECTS OF THE
URBAN PRINCIPALSHIP

Significant recent research suggests that in order to create
and maintain effective and successful schools, the principal must
be actively engaged in instructional leadership. In order to accomplish this task, Hallinger and Murphy (1987) contend that
three conditions must exist. The first is that decision-makers at
the district level must reduce obstacles that inhibit building principals from completing their instructional leadership tasks. The
second condition focuses on defining instructional leadership
in realistic ways to enhance the likelihood that the strategies
will be implemented. The third condition is that assessment
methods "must generate reliable, valid data on instructional leadership behavior and provide information principals can use in
their professional development" (p. 55). The urban principal's
ability to be an instructional leader is critical to any aspect of
success and achievement.

Ways Urban Principals Can Enhance Instruction

Kirby and Colbert (1994) have suggested that principals who empower teachers are likely to enhance the achievement levels at their schools. These researchers examined thirty high schools with regard to faculty empowerment. Thirty principals were examined to determine to what extent they genuinely empowered teachers in their building. The findings of this study suggested that the overall climate of a building changes in direction relation to the level to which the principal empowers teachers. The authors noted, " [t]eachers are not treated as means to their own advancement, but as professionals capable of advancing the vision they share for the school" (p. 48). Essentially, the principal plays a significant role in the instructional process and teachers in the building must believe the principal's desire to effect reform is genuine. The authors believe "[a]ttempts to train current and prospective principals to share leadership responsibilities with teachers may have little impact on the actual governance of schools unless these principals are perceived to act in a genuine manner" (p. 48). Urban principals, like administrators at all other levels, must learn to share governance with teachers and teachers must be responsible in the management of the lives of urban children.

Instructional practices in urban schools are central to any success for urban children. Brookover (1985) identified seven variables that enhance an effective school:

1. School goals and instructional objectives.
   a. School goals, of which the first priority is attaining mastery of identified instructional objectives by all students, are clearly stated.
   b. Standards for mastery of instructional objectives for all students and procedures for certifying attainment of those standards are clearly stated.
   c. Instructional objectives for each grade level are clearly stated and reflect the school's goal of basic skill achievement.

    d. Professional staff recognizes and accepts the priority of mastery of instructional objectives for all students.

2. An effective program of structured direct instruction is incorporated into a mastery learning strategy for achievement of objectives by all students.

3. An orderly, relatively quiet, work-oriented atmosphere reflecting effective school and classroom discipline is established.

4. The instructional program resulting in a high percentage of the total school day should be used as "academic engaged time" for all students.

5. Academic group competition is used to promote peer learning and motivation.

6. Reinforcement principles, contingent upon expected learning conduct, are employed.

7. Assessment data are used effectively.

    a. Ongoing monitoring of student progress is carried out including diagnosis and regular feedback to pupils.

    b. Accurate record keeping of mastery of objectives by all students is required.

    c. Diagnostic information is utilized in planning corrective instruction.

    d. Schoolwide data is used for evaluating and improving the school's instructional program. (p. 265–266).

USING CULTURAL LINKAGES

Firestone and Wilson (1985) have contended that "principals can influence instruction by working through the linkages that govern teacher behavior" (p. 7). The authors provide two approaches to linkages: bureaucratic and cultural. The bureaucratic approach to influencing instruction suggests focusing on at least four areas of instruction, such as schedules, allocation of students to classrooms, budgets, and curriculum. These are obvious influences and organizational decision-making that the principal can use to direct instruction. The bureaucratic aspect of influence can be impacted by a number of variables, including the influence and respect the principal attains, the principal's ability to negotiate for resources, and political influences within the school district.

The major area of focus for urban principals, however, is directed toward cultural linkages. Firestone and Wilson (1985) indicate "cultural linkages work directly on people's consciousness to influence how they think about what they do" (p. 13). This approach to influencing instruction is perhaps the best approach for urban school leaders. Two unique aspects are examined: the first is interpretation of task and the second is the level, or degree, of commitment to tasks. The authors propose "Commitment refers to the individual's willingness to devote energy and loyalty to the organization and the attachment of that person to the organization. It includes a willingness to keep working in the school (continuance commitment), emotional bonds to the school (cohesion commitment), and a willingness to follow the rules and norms governing behavior (control commitment)" (p. 13).

Attention to instruction from a cultural perspective can be enhanced through diversity and trust within the organization. Diversity of faculty and school principals are central factors in improved instruction. It is important to note that icons and rituals are perceived as effective methods principals can use to enhance instruction. The authors suggested that systems of symbols exist and can be used to effectively communicate instructional content to students. They noted that these symbols include stories, icons, and rituals and that these symbols constitute culture, which influences instruction.

EFFECTIVE URBAN PRINCIPALS

Kofi Lomotey's (1989) work on African-American principals provides an excellent overview of qualities associated with being an effective principal and the importance of instructional and academic success in urban environments. He has identified three qualities of effective principals that were analyzed in a 1989 California study:

♦ A commitment to African-American children

♦ A compassion for, and understanding of, their students and of the communities in which they work

♦ Confidence in the ability of all African-American children to learn.

In this study, Lomotey indicated that instructional leadership was a central theme for effective urban principals. He identified areas of involvement such as curriculum planning, attending curriculum-oriented meetings, and staying abreast of curriculum issues. One consistent theme clearly suggested that principals need to be enlightened about their school and children, and that community is key to instructional achievement and success of children (Kanpol and Yeo, 1990).

ATTRACTING WOMEN AND MINORITIES TO BE URBAN PRINCIPALS

Most school organizations with sizable percentages of minorities in the district make consistent public appeals for more minority teachers and administrators. As school districts attempt to diversify their faculty, it is imperative that districts with a significant percentage of minority students make a special effort in recruitment and retention of minority administrators. Some of the questions that should be addressed are as follows: What factors attract women and minorities to become principals? How can these factors be employed to impact achievement of urban students?

Crow and Glascock (1995) referred to a study by Dan Lortie who noted that people are attracted to various occupations because of factors such as money, prestige, and power. The authors propose that little research has been conducted on the reasons why minority professionals and women seek administrative positions. Income and influence are two essential factors. Crow and Glascock noted that while these two essential factors certainly appeal to women and minorities, their traditional roles in today's society discourage women who aspire to these positions.

Women face a number of hurdles in making a transition to the principalship. Historically, most African-American administrators were hired in the South and worked in schools that were all African-American, which received limited resources, such as books and other instructional materials (Pigford and Tonnsen 1993). Charol Shakeshaft (1989) suggests that not only do women face gender barriers in achieving administrative positions, but are also likely to be placed in the lowest administrative ranks within school organizations. There is also considerable evidence to suggest that females are assigned to less desirable buildings. Typically, this means that the female and minority administrators are assigned to buildings with minority populations, less desirable locations, and schools with severe academic and discipline concerns (Revere, 1986). Collins (1998) completed a review of literature regarding female African-American and Caucasian principals and indicated that female African-American principals were usually placed in predominantly African-American urban schools that were experiencing academic and social adjustment issues. As a result, it was suggested that high stress among female principals in these settings may have impacted their ability to become effective leaders.

Some of the challenges that African-American females confront include barriers such as racism and sexism. Other barriers include general employment discrimination, lack of role models, and most recently sexual harassment. One of the more recently discussed aspects of women in principalships, as well as superintendencies, include issues related to competence and administrative skills. There is sufficient evidence in the literature to support the position that women have been marginalized in American society as a whole and there is little evidence to suggest that women experience anything different in school administration.

There is clear evidence that successful urban schools require strong leadership by all members of the school community and especially the building principal. The urban principal must emphasize the following areas: (a) understanding the unique role of culture, (b) focusing on what needs to be accomplished, (c) identifying key individuals' commitment to goal attainment in the building and community, (d) accurately identifying strengths and weaknesses with the school and district, (e) securing political and policy support from the superintendent and board, (f) collaborating with universities and colleges and (g) providing effective ways to evaluate and enhance the principal's performance.

UNDERSTANDING THE UNIQUE ROLE OF CULTURE

Urban principals, regardless of race or ethnicity, must have a comprehensive understanding of the culture that exists within the urban community. This understanding of culture suggests that the urban principals will not allow fear or stereotypes to guide their interactions with urban children and families. They need to have a genuine sense of values, moral and ethical decision-making, and a genuine sense of appreciation and respect for the cultural surroundings of children. Jackson May (1997) indicated that most professionals who are new to an urban environment have not had significant interaction with urban children and have typically been prepared by institutions of higher education that often confirm the stereotypes of urban culture perpetuated by the media and popular culture.

Essential aspects of culture that administrators must learn entail knowledge of the overall urban experiences and a complete rejection of the social-deficit theory regarding school failure. The social-deficit theory contends that children from impoverished communities cannot be successful in school because of inferior home and community life. Essentially, myths and misconceptions that regard the culture in urban communities to be deficient and negative must be destroyed so that principals will plan for positive successes. Urban principals need to demonstrate, in their approaches to children and parents of urban environments, that the students' culture is significant and respected by school policy-makers, and especially by the principal and teachers. Lomotey (1990) noted in his book, *Going to School*, that all educational institutions instill sociocultural values and beliefs in children. He noted that "[s]ocial responsibility, self respect for others, and comfort with one's own cultural background as well as with the background of others are of critical importance" (p. 7).

FOCUS ON WHAT NEEDS TO BE ACCOMPLISHED

The most important internal aspect for administrators to focus on is the need to improve academic achievement. Urban principals must create collaborative relationships with teachers, counselors, students, families, and other community stakeholders who are interested in the academic success of urban children. When an organization faces a number of challenges with significant consequences, organizational needs must be prioritized. This priority should always focus on children.

Assistant principals in urban schools play important roles in establishing priorities because they are likely to be the person who initially interacts with children and adults in the home. Teachers, counselors, and other professionals are important to urban school success as well. With regard to school counselors, Pedersen and Carey (1994) have strongly suggested that culturally competent school counselors play a significant role in the development of racial identity as well as student–teacher interaction. The central theme again focuses on collaboration and interaction of all urban school leaders.

IDENTIFY KEY INDIVIDUALS COMMITTED TO GOAL ATTAINMENT IN THE BUILDING AND COMMUNITY

Urban principals cannot make schools successful by themselves. Any positive, significant change in urban schools will require significant collaboration between teachers' unions, community leaders, parent associations, civic organizations, politicians, and urban children themselves. New urban principals should quickly conduct a "key-individual assessment. A key-individual assessment will identify individuals within the school and community who are central figures to school success. The urban principal should communicate with these individuals immediately and request their support for the community's schools. New parents should be identified and welcomed to the school. The principal should also make an effort to engage new key communicators in the school as well.

It is important for urban principals to identify the specific goals they wish to accomplish and to share how teachers and community members can assist in reaching those goals. The goals should, of course, be mutual and beneficial to urban children. There should be general consensus regarding resources required to achieve the goals. Coalitions should receive updates and reports from the principal and staff regularly. The principal and staff should provide ample opportunities for input and recommendations. These activities should occur throughout the year.

ACCURATELY IDENTIFY STRENGTHS AND WEAKNESSES OF THE SCHOOL AND DISTRICT

Urban principals should be encouraged to recruit committed professionals to work in urban schools. In addition to teacher-selection, urban principals should exercise professional care in the selection of custodians, cooks, librarians and teacher aides, and any other people who interact with school children. All new and continuing personnel should be required to list strengths and weaknesses regarding the schools and the district. These strengths and weaknesses should be substantiated with facts and examples to limit the possibility of rumor or other unsubstantiated comments. It is also important that principals accurately identify both positive and negative aspects of the school. Often, there is a tendency either to overstate or understate incidents, qualities, and characteristics of the urban school.

The media consistently overstate incidents at urban schools. These overstatements perpetuate the stereotype that urban schools are overly violent and academically deficient. Accurately identifying strengths and weaknesses with the school and the district permits a more realistic appraisal of the school and provides a basis for focusing on strategies for improvement.

SECURE POLITICAL AND POLICY-SUPPORT FROM THE SUPERINTENDENT AND SCHOOL BOARD

For many years, school communities assumed that schools were not affected by political actions. The perception was that schools operated at levels where decisions were made purely in the interest of children. Slowly, researchers and practitioners began to realize that schools were social institutions and, therefore, subject to the same influences and challenges as other institutions. Not only are schools bureaucratic but they are political. Much of the political activity, however, occurs at the school board level. Gallagher, Bagin, and Kindred (1997) purported that school boards are used as political power bases and are often dominated by one political party. In describing reform in the Chicago Public Schools, Pink (1992) suggested the evolution of politics was evident on at least four different levels: (a) the politics of business interest in the city, (b) the politics of the State House, (c) the politics of local school governance, and (d) the politics of union activity. Although the principal may be somewhat removed from some of the political variables, the actions and results of incidents or achievements at the building level become the examples and criteria by which decisions are made. In other words, a principal could create a program that was designed to assist students in one school community. The success or failure of the local program, however, could impact political interactions at various political levels.

Politics are a reality for urban principals. Considerable attention should be given to securing political and policy support for the programs organized at the building level. Principals should be cautious with any political contacts and should have consent from the superintendent before contacting political decision-makers. Accurate and fluid communications are essential for urban principals.

COLLABORATION WITH UNIVERSITIES AND COLLEGES

Urban principals should aggressively seek out universities for collaborative endeavors. Many urban school communities have created and maintained effective cooperative efforts with universities. The interactions with universities range from Boston University's takeover of the Chelsea School District to collaborative ventures such as those described by James Comer of New Haven, Connecticut. Other possibilities include establishing professional-development schools, arranging for interns from the university to serve at urban schools, and creating lab/university schools. Partnerships with universities can create meaningful interactions with the urban school. Successful interaction requires that university professors have a genuine interest in working with urban children and that the schools are equal partners in the change process.

PROVIDE EFFECTIVE WAYS TO EVALUATE THE PRINCIPAL'S AND SCHOOL'S PERFORMANCE

Evaluations of principals should be correlated directly to the evaluation of teachers, counselors, custodians, cooks, and other personnel who work in the particular school. While this should not be perceived as a recommendation for the elimination of individual evaluation and assessment of professionals, there should be an evaluation that reviews the overall success of the entire school. It would be advantageous if merit pay and other incentives were directly related to the success as evaluated by parents, children, and other school stakeholders. If the school were truly a collaborative venture, evaluation should also be collaborative. Collaboration must move beyond being a trendy term; collaboration must become reality in urban schools and become an essential tool principals use to bring comprehensive school change to urban communities.

SUMMARY

Pink and Hyde (1992) pointed out that there is no single remedy for all urban schools. Many urban schools and schools in general tend to want to have prepackaged concepts or approaches for school and community improvement. These authors contend there is no one-size-fits-all approach for improving urban schools. Given the intense need to resolve urban school challenges, there is a desire by well-meaning professionals to come up with programs or specialized projects to address specific needs or concerns.

The urban school faces a number of challenges that have been described in the literature. Three contemporary challenges described by Pink (1992) involve the urban principal. Some of the popular proposals are parental choice programs, teacher professionalization, and community empowerment. Parental choice programs demand that principals raise standards of achievement as indicated through competitive measurements determined by the quantity and quality of children who attend a particular school. This is a marketplace approach to urban school management, which might require the principal to become engaged in successfully marketing the school to children and parents.

The second challenge involves teachers and their need to enhance professionalism. Pink suggested that this challenge affects teachers in two ways: (a) teachers have greater responsibilities as schools restructure governance, shifting the decision-making power from the central office to the building or school community; and (b) teachers gain influence on the pedagogical or instructional emphasis regarding "what to teach, how to teach it, and what materials to use when teaching it" (p. 98). Pink noted "concepts such as school-site-based management, school–university partnerships, shared decision making, teacher professionalization, and staff collegiality have been used to describe variants of this improvement strategy" (p. 98).

A third challenge Pink identified focused on community empowerment. Involving and empowering the community has been very attractive to urban administrators and professors of education. This approach emphasizes deinstitutionalization of the urban bureaucracy and redistributing power at the community level. Pink noted, "the logic here is that, because (a) the professional educator is part of the problem, a major contributor to poor schools, then (b) creating good schools can only be accomplished if reforms empower others (in this case parents and the wider community that each school serves) to control the actions of the professional educator" (p. 99).

Although Pink has pointed out significant challenges facing professionals working in the urban environment, there must be a spiritual leadership commitment demonstrated by principals and all other professionals who work in the urban community. This spiritual leadership consists of a genuine interest to work with urban children, an understanding of the history and unique experiences of the group, and an intrinsic appreciation of the environment that exhibits itself in communication and nonverbal interactions with constituents. Spiritual leadership requires a vision that sees beyond what is and moves toward what can be.

6

THE URBAN SUPERINTENDENT

INTRODUCTION

The role of the school superintendent has changed rather significantly over the last fifty years (Sanders, 1996). Sanders noted "in addition to this major social shift, the growing independence of teachers' unions meant that the superintendent now had to delegate a great deal of responsibility and authority to an assistant who would be an independent educational leader but also manage within the leadership constructs of the superintendent" (p. 27). The urban superintendency is a complex job. Because of the sheer size and nature of large systems, it differs from rural and suburban superintendencies. The urban superintendent must be able to adjust to radical change and realize that his or her tenure is likely to be fewer than three years.

This chapter opens with an examination of the role of the urban deputy superintendent as well as an investigation into the nature and scope of the changing superintendency with particular focus on size and complexity of the urban organization. The chapter concludes with special attention to a case-study involving the selection procedures for a non-traditional superintendent and the subsequent internal and external considerations associated with that approach to selecting a school executive.

THE DEPUTY SUPERINTENDENT

It is necessary to briefly examine the urban deputy superintendent as most superintendents ascend to superintendency through the traditional route of being a teacher, a principal, and a central-office staff member (Lunenberg and Ornstein, 1991). The ability of the deputy superintendent to understand and fulfill the directives of the superintendent and board of education are central to the successful accomplishment of the mission of the district. The successful deputy superintendent plays a role in the systemic leadership of the school organization. Crow and Slater (1996) pointed out that "systemic leadership requires the mobilization of the collective ideals . . . . [This] require[s] system-wide and system-pervasive leadership; in short, systemic leadership" (p. 4). This systemic leadership is important for deputy superintendents because given the tenure of urban superintendents, deputy superintendents become likely candidates for a vacant position.

While there is considerable information on effective school principals and valuable data on superintendents is available, there is a dearth of information and data on the role, mission, and responsibilities of the deputy superintendent in large, urban districts. Deputy superintendents perform critical administrative and political roles on behalf of the superintendent and function as the superintendent's immediate executive assistant and administrator. As second-in-command (with formal authority) within the school organization, it is critical to investigate this position from a policy perspective given that the deputy superintendent is responsible for carrying out policies and regulations established by the superintendent and board. The deputy superintendent assists in preparing regulations and instructing school personnel, formulating and administering curricula, supervising school policy, and working directly at the discretion of the superintendent.

A study by Sanders (1997) revealed that urban deputy superintendents aspire to leadership within the district, but are pleased not to have the direct responsibility of a superintendent. Most urban deputy superintendents were highly educated and usually held specific areas of responsibility such as curriculum, personnel, or a school business-related function. Deputy superintendents expressed concerns about their future because they perceived themselves to be linked to the success of the superintendent. Given the turnover rate of superintendents, most urban deputy superintendents expressed concern about "waiting for the right superintendency."

THE URBAN SUPERINTENDENT

In a 1990 survey of United States superintendents, 24 percent of the superintendents in the largest 100 school districts were freshmen superintendents (Ornstein and Levine, 1990). In 1993, slightly over 200 superintendents in the largest districts (over 25,000 students) earned an average of $107,954, with a range of $75,000 to $195,000, with an additional $25,000 to $50,000 in fringe benefits. Although these large districts offer competitive salaries, they are often wrought with enormous challenges. Larry Cuban (1988) noted in his book on urban school superintendents that in 1976 superintendents, especially urban superintendents, were not likely to be men for all seasons. He further described the need for these executives to adjust to radical changes. Cuban noted, "schoolmen did manage to exercise enormous organizational influence through such roles as figurehead of the organization, spokesman of the system, resource allocation, negotiator, crisis-handler, and disseminator of information" (p. 171). Cuban also described the urban superintendency as a vulnerable and insecure expert's job. The superintendency has become a very complex and difficult job for school leaders. Cuban (1988) concluded that the superintendent must accomplish four desired results:

1. Imagine what the organization can become; define the mission; set the goals

2. Motivate peoples' energies toward achieving the organizational goals

3. Link the mission to organizational routines and behaviors

4. Promote certain values that give the organization a distinctive character

Hallinger and Murphy (1988) have identified nine specific tasks necessary for superintendents, which are: staff selection, supervision, staff evaluation, staff development, rewards and sanctions, goals development, resource allocation, monitoring, and forming technical specifications. While all of these tasks are critical, shrinking financial resources make educational leadership even more challenging. Leithwood (1995) pointed out that school executives should focus on curriculum, instruction, teaching, learning, and evaluation.

Ornstein (1992) indicated that only three percent of the nation's superintendents are minorities. However, within the larger context of the 100 largest districts, the percentage is more than twenty percent. This description by Ornstein suggests that the larger districts are somewhat more likely to have a minority as the chief executive officer.

THE CHANGING SUPERINTENDENCY

Most educational leaders agree that the most difficult position in education is the urban school superintendency. Cuban (1970) indicated that size and complexity of the urban community has always been a challenge for superintendents to manage. With high levels of unemployment and difficulty in securing appropriate finances for managing urban schools, the leadership of such organizations requires considerable skills and talents.

While the objectives identified by Larry Cuban (1970) are covered in any university's introductory administration course, these objectives become much more of a challenge for an urban superintendent. The complexity associated with the urban superintendency requires political insight and fiscal skills, in addition to the ability to be all things to all people. Although not officially included on job descriptions for urban superintendents, it could easily be recommended that the urban superintendent be able to "walk on water." Lunenberg and Ornstein (1991) provide an excellent example of urban-school complexities by noting "decisions, which should take days or weeks, often take months or even years, as each department conducts it own reviews and adds its recommendations to be considered by the next level" (p. 331).

THE FEMALE SUPERINTENDENT

Historically, the primary role of women was domestic. Her roles and responsibilities outside the home were limited. Tyack and Strober (1981) indicated that women taught their families in the home and in dame schools. By the end of the 18th century, young women were hired to teach young children during the summer in one-room schools. The early rationale women proposed to encourage more women to pursue careers in education was that women possessed certain attributes, which were said to be endowed by God. They stated women are: (a) nurturing, (b) patient, (c) able to understand young minds, and (d) exemplary in moral influence (Tyack and Strober (1981)). Urban-school teaching salaries were two to three times higher than rural salaries, women outnumbered men ten to one, and taught primarily in the lower grades while men served as managers and principals in the higher grades.

Despite affirmative action policies, women have faced significant struggles to equalize their numbers compared to men in key school leadership positions (Grady, 1995). The research indicates significant historical opposition to women becoming school leaders. In terms of the superintendency, there has been consistent underrepresentation of females (Tallerico, Burstyn, and Poole 1993). For example, according to the American Association of School Administrators, women held 1.3 percent of all superintendencies in 1994 (Blount, 1995). Current data suggests that women constitute approximately 5.6 percent of the superintendents in the nation. According to Chase (1995), there are an average of twelve female superintendents per state. These low numbers cause female superintendents to be isolated from each other and limit gender-consistent feedback and support.

Rosener (1995) reported that women have been moving from lower- to middle-management, but have not been successful at securing chief executive officerships in business and education. In fact, Rosener believes that the overall status of women in key, executive leadership positions has not changed in the last fifteen years. She specifically looked at 100 female and male managers. The females overwhelmingly indicated they were not fully utilized because of their gender. Male mangers did not express this concern. Rosener's findings appear to be consistent with

Grogan (1996), who indicated that the position of the superintendency has experienced significant change in the last fifty years, yet the public perception has not changed and most of the public continues to view the superintendency as a male occupation.

Female leaders who have become superintendents are usually very high achievers and have dominant personalities (Genzen, 1993). Brunner (1994) believes that females identify power as an important element in becoming and remaining a superintendent and that female superintendents share the following characteristics. They tend to:

♦ Demonstrate strong senses of efficacy; they believe they can do anything they decide to do.

♦ Secure strong support from one or more men when achieving career goals; men are needed to actively campaign in favor of gender diversity.

♦ Be extremely bright, not be openly ambitious, be workaholics, retain gender identity in a conservative, normative sense, and be exceptionally skillful.

♦ Be solitary, because the majority of their colleagues are men.

♦ Dedicate themselves to the care of children.

♦ Practice survival skills, in the way they dress, in achieving doctoral degrees, in their willingness to work eighty-hour weeks, in cultivating connections to power networks in the community, and in recognizing the necessity of having male advocates when applying for positions.

♦ Use collaboration where one person is not more powerful than another. They practice approaches to power that stress collaboration, inclusion, and consensus-building.

♦ Believe in God. Their attainment of the superintendency was believed to be part of a larger deity's plan.

The female superintendent in urban environments has not been studied to a large degree; however, researchers such as Barbara Jackson (1995) of Fordham University have devoted their careers to examining underrepresented females in the role of the superintendent. Again, from an urban perspective, the issues confronting female superintendents are more extensive, complicated, and require responses to numerous constituent groups.

CASE STUDY: A CHALLENGE TO THE URBAN SUPERINTENDENCY

Evidence supports the position that superintendents are no longer father figures who dispense knowledge among students and teachers; rather superintendents must focus on the interaction of individuals who represent various groups within the school organization. As a result of this interaction, the superintendent must assume myriad roles as the educational leader. Recent evaluations of superintendents' leadership skills have been questioned by boards of education across the country. The intense scrutiny and constant evaluation of superintendents by boards of education has led some districts to break the long standing educational tradition of hiring school executives who have been promoted through the administrative ranks. They seek chief executive officers who are hired by and work for private businesses. Executives hired by businesses report almost exclusively to the firm and not to the local board of education. Furthermore, the executive in charge of the school district often does not have a degree or in education or educational administration.

Traditionally, school boards have identified the superintendent as the individual who will lead and serve as the principal visionary for the school organization. However, given the demands placed on the superintendent and the board, non-traditional options are being considered by school boards. Many school districts are opting to employ a superintendent who has a business- or industrial-management background. The following case analysis (Sanders, Patterson-Stewart, Jackson May,

Ludwig, Plummer, and Salazar-Valentine (1998)) provides a complete picture of a large Midwestern board of education that opted to pursue a non-traditional candidate as the superintendent and considered hiring a business firm to manage the schools.

BACKGROUND OF THE CASE STUDY

This case study utilized the interview-guide format of qualitative research and included five board members from a large Midwestern urban school district. The interview-guide included a list of questions and issues that explored specific issues associated with the selection of a firm to manage the district in place of a traditional superintendent. The formatted interview was particularly beneficial because of the singularly focused issue under investigation. The intent of this research was to provide a focused perspective on one issue, yet permit each board member flexibility to provide additional information on the subject. The following information provides an overview of the school district and the major issues board members identified.

OVERVIEW OF THE SCHOOL DISTRICT

Investigators studied a large Midwestern city school district currently educating approximately 40,000 students with approximately 49 percent of the school district classified as minority. The district's largest minority group is African-American. It is the fourth largest school district in the state and, like many school districts around the country, the board of education faced the retirement of their superintendent. (There are predictions that by the turn of the century, there could be at least a fifty percent turnover in school superintendents). The retiring superintendent was an "insider" who had devoted over thirty years of his career to the district. He attended a nearby, respected educational university and by all accounts was a popular superintendent, who enjoyed bipartisan racial support. The "inside" superintendent had the unique ability to successfully communicate with all groups within the community and during his tenure as superintendent, there were no reported issues of racial stress. In addition to being the first African-American superintendent in the history of the school district, he was supported by the board as well as ethnic and racial pockets in the community.

As a result of the superintendent's announced retirement, the board of education and other community members identified a list of qualities for the new superintendent. The number-one criteria identified by the board and thirty community members was for the new superintendent to have the ability to make their urban schools the number-one urban district in the country. (The desire to become the number-one urban school district is probably a similar criterion boards of education throughout the country list as a high priority.) The board hired the McKenzie Group of Washington, D.C., to conduct a national search for a superintendent. (The McKenzie Group is a consulting firm that specializes in recruiting urban superintendents. The last time this urban board of education had conducted a national search for a superintendent had been over twenty years ago.

THE BUSINESS PERSPECTIVE

The local chamber of commerce, which had maintained a long-standing relationship with the schools, appointed an education committee, Coalition for Effective Education, to review the status of schools and provide feedback regarding the qualities and characteristics for the new superintendent. This group of businesspersons implemented a city-wide survey and found that the community was concerned about the way the district operated and about what the district should look for in a new superintendent. The chamber of commerce strongly recommended to the board that they consider a non-traditional superintendent—perhaps someone with solely a business background who would take a very "business-like" approach to managing the schools. Therefore, when the McKenzie Group was contracted in April 1996 to conduct a nation-wide search, a major part of their responsibility was to investigate non-traditional candidates. The McKenzie Group informed the board that they were largely responsible for recruiting traditional candidates to the superintendency, but would also advertise in non-traditional journals for a superintendent of schools. As part of their search for non-traditional candidates, the search firm accepted forty-two candidates to succeed the retiring superintendent. In addition to the candidates, one board member received information on a professional firm that managed school districts. Ultimately, because of irreconcilable differences between state public disclosure laws and McKenzie group policies regarding confidentiality, the school board determined to conduct its own search.

Information about a Minnesota-based firm, Public Strategies Group (PSG), was made available to one school board member. PSG, a company that manages school districts for profit, provided information to the board members regarding their professional, business-like approach to managing schools. As a result, the board maintained two options: the traditional search for a superintendent and the non-traditional route that PSG represented.

CONSIDERATIONS FOR THE MANAGEMENT FIRM

Unlike a number of urban districts across the country, the large Midwestern school district had a strong financial base, though there was concern about the infrastructure and the need for improved technology throughout the district. The board members were asked why they would consider using a business to manage the schools. The rationale for exploring PSG was to consider an "alternative and non-traditional approach to school management." One of the newer board members noted, "the consideration of the firm was to shake things up because there was a perception that the district needed restructuring and change." All board members indicated that urban schools "are at the crisis stage," but considered the district less troubled than larger urban districts. As a result of this crisis, the school board was looking for anything new and different. Because public schools accept all students, the need to provide for everyone led to a desperate attempt to "be all things to all people."

Several board members indicated they experienced "clear pressure by the business community to make schools operate more efficiently." The pressure on the board to consider non-traditional options was a major factor in the selection of the superintendent. One possible option discussed was to follow an option similar to Seattle's decision to hire a retired general to be superintendent of schools. One board member noted, "there was a general attitude of looking for something different." It appears that the chamber of commerce and the business community as a whole found PSG appealing because of its focus on objectivity and performance-based perspectives. A board member indicated that the business community felt the PSG was close to the way they [the business community] operated and viewed the business-like approach in a very positive manner.

ROLES AND RESPONSIBILITIES OF THE MANAGEMENT FIRM

PSG was to operate like a professional business. The firm was to have a board of directors who would hire the superintendent and the superintendent essentially would be a partner in the firm. This superintendent would then report directly to the board of directors, who would present information and reports to the local board of education. The firm would take a performance-based approach and the achievement of the goals would be mutually established by the board and the firm. According to one board member, "the yardstick by which success would be measured would be established by the board."

PSG operated one school district in Minneapolis, Minnesota, and provided data to the board regarding the success it was experiencing. PSG also provided data that compared Minneapolis with the community in question so board members could draw appropriate comparisons. Based on interviews with the five board members, the firm identified at least sixteen actions they would accomplish immediately:

1. Hire a superintendent
2. Establish a contractual arrangement for the superintendent to become a partner in the firm
3. Work collaboratively with the superintendent for one year
4. Establish a list of incentives that amounted to roughly $400,000 per year

5. Establish measurable objectives by which the success of the firm would be measured

6. Provide agreements to allow for the contract to be canceled at any time by either party

7. Develop a team of leaders within the district

8. Develop a strategic plan

9. Conduct a curriculum audit

10. Develop an action plan

11. Identify student achievement as the major criteria for success

12. Establish benchmarks and baselines for achievement

13. Teach curriculum and instructional assessment

14. Enhance board members' leadership and development skills

15. Implement site-based management

16. Increase family involvement in school decisions

The roles and responsibilities of the firm would be determined by the firm and the local school board. The performance of the firm would essentially determine the salary and merit increases per year.

ADVANTAGES OF THE FIRM

The board identified and agreed upon the following advantages to hiring the firm. There was general agreement regarding the advantages of the firm. One board member could not find any significant advantages to using the business firm.

♦ The firm's operation would be strictly performance-based, according to a signed, legally binding contract. The contract involved the firm meeting expectations established jointly by the board and the firm.

♦ The firm would maintain a methodological approach to school management. The goals and objectives of the firm were clearly described. One board member noted "they had a measured-progress approach to running the schools."

♦ The firm would reorganize the district with a new team of leaders. "These leaders would bring fresh ideas and a new way of doing things" indicated one board member.

♦ The firm represented "change." It was a new look at top-level management and PSG was perceived to be knowledgeable about financial and curricular matters.

♦ The firm was viewed as being the opposite of the traditional bureaucracy. "It wasn't going to be business as usual with the firm." The firm was perceived as bringing a new vitality to the district that would engender interest and respect from the business community."

♦ One of the perceived advantages of the firm was its ability to address grave financial concerns. "The firm basically made the hard financial decisions and then would return the district to the local school board."

♦ PSG was viewed as able to divest some of the strong union contract language.

♦ The business community and the teacher's union were in favor of hiring PSG to manage the school district.

DISADVANTAGES OF THE MANAGEMENT FIRM

Board members identified the following disadvantages to hiring PSG. There was unanimous agreement regarding the disadvantages of the business firm. No order or rank is attached to these disadvantages.

♦ The firm was viewed as an "outsider to the community."

♦ The cost of $400,000 annually to an organization outside the state was viewed extremely negatively. The board received input from the community that it did not want its tax dollars going to another state.

♦ The board noted that the firm employed no persons of color. PSG did not employ any members from a racial minority. This was viewed negatively by the board, which served a student constituency that was nearly fifty percent African-American.

♦ Test scores of minority students in the district the firm was managing were not increasing at a acceptable rate.

♦ The board would have to seek special permission from the legislature to hire someone as superintendent who did not hold a superintendent's certificate/license.

♦ There was some confusion regarding the new role of the local board of education. Since the firm would hire a partner as the superintendent and that partner would report to PSG's board, who would then report to the local board of education? Roles and responsibilities were not clearly defined.

♦ There was expressed concern that PSG possessed limited knowledge about the history of the community.

♦ Some concern was expressed about treating kids as numbers. Because the firm would take a methodological approach to management, one board member expressed concern over the lack of "the personal touch."

COMMUNITY RESPONSE

Two school board members traveled to Minneapolis to visit the management firm and the schools it operated. There was overwhelming agreement that the superintendent/partner in the Minneapolis district was outstanding and was a fine representative of the district. The purpose of the visit was to observe the more intricate aspects of the firm's management approach. The two board members who visited Minneapolis agreed that the visit was beneficial and felt very strongly that PSG would be a positive decision for their urban district.

One major difficulty the board encountered was deciding how it would convey information about PSG to the community. Although there was a thirty-member board with a wide range of community representatives, there was concern about how the firm would function and how the local board would collaborate with the out-of-town firm. The board arranged several pubic hearings in various sections of the community to explain the role of the firm as well as discuss the procedure for selecting a new superintendent.

Segments of the African-American community expressed concern about the management firm taking over the district. Much of this concern, according to board members, was due to the lack of minority representation in the firm and the lagging achievement scores of minority students in PSG's Minneapolis school district. One board member indicated "that the community perceived that the entire district was being privatized, but this was not the case." PSG conceded that they were not pleased with their track record with minority improvement, but that they were working on it. Also, PSG did not report its student achievement data by race and was unable to provide comparative information to citizens.

Another segment of the community, active in the debate regarding the selection of the superintendent, was a group organized for local responsible education. This group of parents was organized to provide a recommendation for the superintendent. The group developed its own criteria for the selection of the superintendent. There was some confusion regarding what happened to the recommendations.

THE FINAL DECISION

A preliminary assessment of the board revealed that there was support of PSG by a vote of four to one; however, there were at least three major reasons the firm was not selected. Perhaps the most significant reason for rejecting PSG's proposal was the result of the board's inquiry regarding the legal ramifications associated with hiring a firm as opposed to a traditional superintendent. State statutes indicated that boards of education could only hire superintendents who possessed a current state superintendent's certificate, which required a minimum of sixty-four semester hours in educational administration, management, curriculum, and human foundations.

The second reason the firm was not selected was a result of the lack of minority representation in the firm and the lack of sufficient progress of minority achievement scores. Segments of the African-American community loudly objected to the firm due to the lack of minority representation.

The third reason the board rejected PSG was the public perception that a large sum of money was going to a firm located outside of the community and the state and the perception that PSG would feel little accountability to the community. The firm proposed charging approximately $400,000 per year. It was unclear whether the firm would be more concerned with making a profit than with working with children.

There was also a political component to the decision as well. The school board would likely have had to place a levy on the ballot during the fall of 1997. There was apprehension that the community's concern about the outside firm would not be perceived as an asset when the community was asked to vote.

This case study is significant because it could represent a growing trend in school leadership in the new millennium. Urban schools are searching for answers to the challenges that seem to have no answers. Given that some communities have a growing interest in managing schools like businesses and in turning to management firms to operate their schools, the selection of a non-traditional school executive may be cause for concern by educators throughout the nation.

FUTURE CONSIDERATIONS AND RECOMMENDATIONS FOR THE NON-TRADITIONAL SCHOOL EXECUTIVE

We asked the board about future considerations regarding the use of management firms to replace the traditional superintendent. The board appeared to be very attracted to the contemporary leadership concepts some graduate educational programs are currently teaching. The board seemed to respond to five benefits the management firm offered: (a) shared decision making, (b) measured objectives, (c) resource allocation, (d) rewards for performance, and (e) contractual consensus for merit.

The major attraction for the firm was its objectivity and methodological approach. Future boards selecting superintendents will likely use contracts that are increasingly more performance- and merit-based. A popular position is that if there is a movement for school boards to reform and to become more responsible for achievement, they will increase accountability and responsibility for the superintendent.

Additional thought should be focused on the psychology of management firms and the perceptions of school administrators. School principals and staff members are still developing opinions regarding the business-management paradigm and education. The age-old argument about whether it is possible to operate a human resource organization like a business is still prevalent. The attraction of some business-management practices is appropriate in educational administration, but other perspectives must be maintained.

SUMMARY

The urban superintendency is a complex, multifaceted position. It requires that the school executive have an appreciation of a number of internal and external factors that impact the success of the school organization. While the superintendency is changing, there are yet elements of this position that have not changed. The urban superintendency of the next century will be more political and will include more fundraising and related community functions. The urban superintendent will become more like a college president who is required to satisfy board members and raise funds through means other than referendums.

Women are likely to play a larger role in urban superintendencies in the future. In addition to women ascending to superintendencies, there will also likely be additional focus on selecting non-traditional candidates. The successful urban superintendent must be able to establish political affiliations and seek support external to the organizations while maintaining strong public support for reform.

7

THE URBAN SCHOOL BOARD

Local school boards are an essential and enduring part of the American institution of representative government. Directly accountable to the people, local school boards are the educational policy makers for the public schools in the local communities. They are advocates for local public education with other local, state, and federal governmental entities.

National School Boards Association:
Resolutions Beliefs and Policies
Constitution and Bylaws (1997)

INTRODUCTION

The role and purpose of the American school board as a governing body has recently faced some rather serious challenges. For example, Danzberger (1994) suggested that it is the school boards' turn to take some of the criticism often directed toward superintendents, principals, teachers, and children. Danzberger's position is shared by other practitioners and researchers who have concluded that the reform movement has essentially overlooked the importance of the governing body. Practitioners such as Davis Campbell and Diane Green (1994) and researchers such as Plank, Scotch, and Gamble (1996) and Hill (1994) all indicate that change in the governance structure of schools is the next logical step for reform.

The purpose of this chapter is to describe contemporary issues faced by urban school boards. The chapter will further describe the process and the nature of the interaction between the board and internal and external constituencies within the community. This information will focus rather exclusively on school practitioners and school board members in terms of the unique challenges faced by school boards. Recommendations for school districts that are considering non-traditional alternatives to traditional school executives are provided.

GOVERNANCE ISSUES IN URBAN EDUCATION

A school board is a unique elected body; there is probably no other social institution in which a governing body can receive a complaint and act upon it immediately. Moreover the school board has the power and authority to impact immediate change. The governance of American education is an example of the only American institution where the people make decisions and the results are expected to be immediate. Russo (1992) noted that the traditional school board authority is grounded in first-generation origins of colonial Massachusetts. Russo explores the paradox of school board leadership and suggests "that while local boards as the governing bodies of school districts are agents of the state responsible for local education, they are not free to exercise unfettered discretion on behalf of their local constituencies; they must act as parameters established by the state" (p. 3).

According to Michael Kirst (1994), co-director of Policy Analysis for California Education, there are simply too many school boards (about 15,000) and too many school-board members (about 97,000). Because of the size of this population, research is often difficult and typically reflects only a portion of the population. Any analyses, therefore, have limitations in terms of recommendations and policies. Kirst suggests that historically, the last major change in school-board organization occurred between 1910 and 1920. The nature of this change focused on decentralization and a "ward committee" style of management. The ward committee operated somewhat in a vacuum and focused almost exclusively on issues that were unique to their own geographic areas. Danzberger and Usdan (1994) indicated that this was the period when the school board changed from being an operating-oriented board to a policy board. These authors further indicated that "the blurring of the roles of the superintendent and the board makes it difficult to define the locus of accountability for policy and administration and intensifies the pressures that constituents exert on members of boards to become little more than purveyors of constituent services" (p. 366). This blurring of the roles was a departure from the perceived centralized bureaucratic model of school governance that was almost exclusively dominated by men. Kirst (1994) noted "the governance structure needed to be revised so that school boards would be small, elected at-large, and purged of all connections with political parties and officials of general government, such as mayors and councilmen" (p. 379).

SCHOOL BOARD COMPLEXITY

At the beginning of the twentieth century, school reformers attempted to model school-board governance after that of big corporations (Kirst, 1994). It was during this period that boards began to combine legislative, judicial, and executive responsibilities and essentially created a more complex school governance structure.

The legislative aspects of the board's governance is demonstrated when they "adopt budgets, pass regulations, and set policies" (p. 379). Kirst suggests that school boards further operate as a legislative organization because they provide constituent-services and respond to parental requests regarding specific issues that must be addressed. Kirst noted that "parents phone board members about fixing showers in the locker rooms, relocating school crossing guards, and reclassifying children placed in special education (p. 379).

School boards are also responsible for judicial concerns regarding student appeals such as suspensions, pupil distribution, and expulsion hearings. The board is also involved in hearing appeals from teaching, administrative, and staff members at all levels. Kirst noted that "after all administrative remedies are exhausted, the board is the final body for appeal, though citizens may still turn to the courts in some cases" (p. 379).

The complexity of the responsibilities of the school board is further validated by the board's involvement in executive decision-making. The board must approve the district budget as well as every expenditure and contract. Boards are also responsible for the appointment of the superintendent as well as all administrators and teachers. These executive decisions involving millions of dollar are made daily by board members throughout the country. Perhaps this complexity has been described best by Maureen DiMarco, a former California school board member, when she noted the following:

> Take another look at what a school district and school board members are. My colleagues and I are the members of a five member board of directors of a $190 million annual corporation. We are responsible for 4,500 employees at 67 different plants. We negotiate annually with four different unions. We're responsible for 38,000 student units of production on an annual basis, but we have a 13 year production cycle, rarely with any of those products staying with our company for the entire length of time. We have no control over our raw materials. We have to take all of them in the numbers in which they arrive, and all of products go out to the marketplace because we have no backroom in which to discard our flawed and damaged merchandise (Campbell & Green, 1994, p. 392).

This sentiment illustrates the nature of the complexity associated with school boards across the country. How does a large urban district control an ever-growing budget with continually limited resources? What qualities or characteristics should the board look for in selecting a new superintendent? With the average tenure of an urban superintendent at less than three years, what action should take place that will enhance the professional relationship between superintendents and school boards?

SCHOOL BOARD CHALLENGES

There are two main perspectives regarding the paradox of school board control: one perspective suggests that some change or reform is critically needed; the second perspective maintains that boards do not need radical reform, but need high-quality leaders. Considerable research and policy focus on the challenges school boards face. The following challenges to school boards are discussed in this chapter: (a) school board reform, (b) financial limitations (faced by school boards and superintendents), and (c) school board transitions.

SCHOOL BOARD REFORM

"Reform" is used quite often in educational circles, for reform is necessary and requires a significant focus. Communities, school boards, superintendents, and educators must focus on institutional changes, the need to redesign school organizations, and the need to consider changes in decision-making at all school levels. There has been a great deal of attention in recent years on the need to examine school boards and their need to reform. G. Alfred Hess (1995) provided a unique look at school reform in the Chicago Public Schools. Hess contends that a great number of school reform issues can be traced to the release of *A Nation at Risk* in 1983. This now-famous report essentially suggested that mediocrity was the rule of the day in schools throughout the nation. Following this report a number of states and local school boards began to take a more critical look at areas of achievement and the need to restructure schools. While restructuring typically focused on students, teachers, and administrators, school boards were essentially exempt from the restructuring efforts. Hess (1995) identified three strategies that were employed to accomplish the restructuring effort in Chicago: (a) enhancing teacher professionalism, (b) using market pressure to improve schools via enrollment choice, and (c) involving parents through school-based management.

According to Hess (1995), increasing teacher professionalism entails a number of concepts "from reshaping the preparation of teachers in schools of education, to retraining the entire teaching faculty of a city such as Pittsburgh, to giv[ing] teachers a share of the decision making at local schools under the image of total quality management" (p. 27). The second strategy focused on programs that are still being debated by a number of urban and mid-sized districts. Challenging and controversial issues such as vouchers and block grants from the federal government are part of the efforts to restructure schools and the delivery of education. The third strategy, focused on programs intended to increase parental involvement, many of which were mandated by Title One funds. Parent advisory councils were created and ultimately played a significant role in restructuring schools in Chicago.

In order to support the restructuring schools in Chicago, the Board of Education passed the Chicago School Reform Act in 1988. Hess (1995) identified the ten specific goals for school reform:

1. Assuring that students achieve proficiency in reading, writing, mathematics, and higher order thinking that equals or surpasses national norms;

2. Assuring that students attend school regularly and graduate from high school at rates that equal or surpass national norms;

3. Assuring that students are adequately prepared for further education and aiding students in making a successful transition to further education;

4. Assuring that students are adequately prepared for successful entry into employment and aiding students in making a successful transition to employment;

5. Assuring that students are, to the maximum extent possible, provided with a common learning experience that is of high academic quality and that reflects high expectations for all students to learn;

6. Assuring that students are better prepared to compete in the international market place by having foreign language proficiency and stronger international studies;

7. Assuring that students are encouraged in exploring potential interests in fields such as journalism, drama, art, and music;

8. Assuring that individual teachers are granted the professional authority to make decisions about instruction and the method of teaching;

9. Assuring that students are provided the means to express themselves creatively and to respond to the artistic expression of others through the visual arts, music, drama and dance; and

10. Assuring that students are provided adequate athletic programs that encourage pride and positive identification with the attendance center and that reduce the number of dropouts and teenage delinquents (p. 37-38).

While the reforms listed in the Chicago Reform Act of 1988 are not new, it is interesting to note that there are no provisions or statements about what school boards should do to restructure or focus on the future. Once again, the school board either perceives that it is above the need to restructure or it refuses to acknowledge any role in the current challenges facing urban education.

On a much more practical note, Cronin (1992) suggested that urban school reform for the twentieth century has had three purposes:

1. To protect the city school from patronage, bribery (e.g., by textbook suppliers), and other irregularities in administrative promotion and business management. (Ward politicians and mayors from time to time treated urban schools the same way as they treated sewer and trolley contracts—as sources of jobs for supporters and wealth in the form of kickbacks).

2. To fix responsibility for employment and for purchasing on a relatively small, easily observed board of incorruptible citizens who should hire top educational executive talent on an impersonal merit system.

3. To assimilate immigrant children into the norms and work ethic of prior generations, using the schools as the major tool of socialization and social control (p. 38).

These pragmatic issues Cronin discusses suggest that in order for reform to have any significant impact, there must be some focus on the internal issues of the board itself, given the nature of the bureaucracy within urban schools. While there are exclusive answers to addressing reform in urban schools, there is a need to address both the idealistic as well as the pragmatic challenges that are ahead in the Twenty-first century.

FINANCIAL CHALLENGES FACED BY BOARDS

Without question, the most critical issue school boards face is the challenge of financial management. Miron and Wimpelberg (1992) cited the New Orleans schools as an example of a school system faced with critical financial issues. Due to Louisiana's funding changes in the minimum foundation formula, New Orleans schools would be unable to increase the low rate of $32 per-pupil funding for texts and materials. This example is probably common throughout the country. Other challenges include legal issues, unfunded mandates by state and national policymakers, and issues regarding governance.

"The concern for money is universal in urban education" (Kowalski, 1995, p. 75). All school districts face diminishing resources, but financial stability experienced by urban districts tends to be an issue that requires immediate attention. Financial integrity is so significant that a number of districts are faced with takeovers from mayors (as with the Cleveland City Schools) or by state departments of education (such as the Compton City Schools in California). Kowalski noted that "we see that superintendents cite a lack of financial resources as their greatest problem and financial considerations as the primary factor in decision making" (p. 75). The pervasiveness of financial support for urban districts and superintendents makes it extremely difficult to offer appropriate programming to meet student needs.

Donna Harrington-Lueker, senior editor of the American School Board Journal (1993) indicated that the Twentieth Century Fund/Danforth Foundation's report, *Facing the Challenge*, issued a very strong indictment of the governance of local school boards. The report made several recommendations including the following:

♦ Limiting the school board's role and responsibilities to policymaking, rather than including the board in day-to-day administrative issues

♦ Redefining boards as local, education-policy boards

♦ Hiring outside experts to help local boards solve problems

♦ Holding board elections the same time general elections are held

♦ Refusing to certify any election if fewer than twenty percent of registered voters turn out

SCHOOL BOARD TRANSITIONS

Another example of the challenges school boards face that is particularly significant for urban schools is the transitional nature of school boards. Bennett (1991) provided an example of the unique issues urban boards face by indicating "urban boards are especially at risk: Their behavior lies directly under the watchful eyes of major urban newspapers—linked to wire services that serve the nation" (p. 23). Bennett suggests that urban boards have endured three metamorphoses. "The 1960's and the early 70's saw the waning of the civic-minded urban board member" (p. 23). In "[t]he early 70's the number of minorities and women on urban boards began to increase" (p. 23), thus marking the second phase. Bennett indicates that these two groups shared the common interest of being civic-minded and exhibiting strong commitments to educational service. School boards in the third stage were identified as being clearly political bodies, without special interest. "This board behaves like any other political office holder, concerned primarily with re-election or higher political office and paying assiduous attention to serving political constituents" (p. 23). In many urban districts, the school board is often viewed as a stepping stone to more significant political office. This stepping-stone approach is an unfortunate reality in many school districts and must be avoided, if true reform is to be effective. The responsibility of the urban community is to raise a collective voice against individuals elected to school boards who do not maintain the best interests of the school children. Urban school boards are continuing to experience transition and change. Effective boards in the twenty-first century will have to focus exclusively on meeting the challenges in a collaborative sense and dispense with political infighting.

SUMMARY

It is abundantly clear that there are serious challenges to boards of education and these challenges are likely to increase. The degree to which boards of education address these issues largely depends on the hiring of appropriate personnel to lead the district. That is, the hiring of the chief executive officer of the school district becomes an essential ingredient to any level of school success or effectiveness.

As we progress toward the twenty-first century, there is a crucial need to reexamine all aspects of education. It is time to take a more critical look at the role, purpose, and function of school boards. Fortunately, a number of researchers and practitioners are focusing more attention on governance issues and specifically on the future of boards of education. The issue of power and influence of the boards of education will have to be examined. One of the reasons school boards are considering management firms and nontraditional superintendents is the growing concern for accountability and achievement of students.

It is also critical for urban school boards to eliminate individual agendas of members and to focus on collaborative decision-making and genuine shared governance. Conflict that will inevitably arise in school-related concerns should be handled in a professional, fair manner and the superintendent and board should demonstrate high levels of trust and open communication.

It is also important for controversial issues to be dealt with in a public manner so that the public has current and correct information. The need for open and correct information is especially urgent for underrepresented groups within large cities who may rightly distrust complex bureaucracies. It has often been noted in the literature that conflict and sources of stress tend to be more intensified in urban districts than in county, rural, or suburban districts. Much of the stress or friction that superintendents face was identified by Kowalski (1995) who suggested that "the most common sources of friction between school boards members and superintendents [are] the differing values and beliefs of their respective roles" (p. 47). Values and beliefs regarding board members' roles are not unique to urban districts, but again in larger districts, these issues are intensified, especially when there are at least two newspapers in the city.

McCloud & McKenzie (1994) suggested that most of the difficulties between urban superintendents and school boards center around role-identification and poor levels of communication. These issues are also exacerbated when urban school districts are routinely threatened with takeover by a state educational agency or a city mayor. Recently, the Cleveland Schools were ordered to report to Mayor Michael White. The mayor will now be responsible for appointing school board members. This action is the result of advanced conflict and tension between politicians at the local and state level, and the Cleveland Teacher's Union.

The most important thing for school leaders to remember is that all actions and behaviors should be based on what is in the best interest of children in urban schools. The fact that almost seventy percent of the children attending urban schools live in poverty must be a concern for school leaders. School boards and superintendents need to redesign programs that focus on the needs of the people who genuinely need the most support.

The role of the urban school board and the role of the superintendent are changing—for the better we hope. Changes in progress notwithstanding, students are now being ill served by their schools, problems in urban schools are real today, and solutions must be found now, championed by those who genuinely care about humanity.

RECOMMENDATIONS FOR PRACTICE FOR URBAN SCHOOL LEADERS

The following recommendations are for urban school leaders regarding the internal components of the urban school, specifically addressing teachers, principals, superintendents, and school boards.

♦ Resources for staff development and professional enhancement opportunities should be made available for urban teachers. Opportunities for graduate work, seminars, workshops, and academies that focus on working with urban school populations should be encouraged.

♦ Teachers salaries should be increased. The increase in teacher salaries would encourage more qualified candidates to consider teaching as a career option as well as demonstrate support and appreciation for teachers already in the classroom.

♦ Urban teachers who create weekend academies and special learning opportunities for at-risk students should receive an additional stipend in support of those activities, much like schools currently pay athletic coaches and curriculum advisors.

♦ Teachers who have professional development plans that include exposure to urban communities regarding values, norms, behaviors, characteristics, and related relevant content should be encouraged to consider administrative careers.

♦ Competency based exams should be established that focus specifically on working with urban school children. These exams would be both academic based and have a qualitative affective component.

♦ Collaborative strategies between urban teachers, principals, superintendents, and school boards should be encouraged. Merit and related incentives should be created and supported for programs that create and document their success.

♦ Graduate programs in educational administration should have content related to urban populations and focus specifically on the issues, challenges, and success factors in these communities.

♦ Urban principals should have support personnel to assist with paperwork, reports, and related routine activities in the school environment. This would allow principals to focus on school improvement efforts with teachers, parents, and community leaders.

♦ Incentive programs should be created to encourage urban principals and superintendents to meet high academic expectations for children. Specifically, contracts should be written with incentive clauses and procedures for personal and professional development if the goals are not met.

♦ Teachers, principals, superintendents, and school boards should have community service requirements as part of their contract and evaluation. This community service would require these leaders to document and validate activities, programs, and interactions with the urban community.

♦ Urban school leaders should have evaluations and assessments that describe how they know school culture and climate, share governance, understand program development, and motivate students. This process would include teachers as well as administrators.

8

COMMUNITY RELATIONS AND POLITICS IN URBAN SCHOOLS AND COMMUNITIES

INTRODUCTION

This chapter will reflect on the importance of community relations and politics in urban school organizations and communities. This reflective approach will allow readers to review both empirical studies and anecdotal experiences. The chapter will specifically analyze the following:

♦ The importance of community relations in urban school communities

♦ The relationship model: home, school, and community interaction

♦ The internal and external aspects of the community

♦ The political nature of urban schools and courses of political engagement

♦ The issues surrounding charter schools and vouchers

155

THE IMPORTANCE OF COMMUNITY RELATIONS IN URBAN-SCHOOL COMMUNITIES

Administrators in public schools quickly learn that communication is the lifeblood of their existence. Often, the degree to which administrators and policies are successful is directly related to successful communication strategies. The jobs of urban school leaders are complex and involve a number of tasks. These tasks include setting objectives, organizing tasks, motivating employees, reviewing results, making decisions, and coordinating program and policy reviews. As a result of the high number of tasks assigned to urban school leaders, these tasks cannot be accomplished, or the objectives achieved, without an adequate communication plan.

Urban school leaders, like other administrators, spend about eighty percent of their time communicating with their constituents (Gallagher, Bagin, and Kindred, 1997). The ability to communicate effectively a vision, plan, directive, or policy is literally dependent upon the leader's interpersonal and human-relations skills. In most school organizations, it appears that communication normally flows from the top down. In other words, the people who typically have to enforce or implement a program or strategy are often "given" information in the form of a directive, program guideline, state or district policy, a board-of-education initiative, or new administrative procedure (Hanson, 1996). According to Hanson, much of the feedback that occurs is in the form of summary reports, resource requests, evaluation information, or curricular documents. Therefore, it is critically important for urban school leaders to be aware of verbal and nonverbal communication characteristics that could result in support for or opposition to the organization. In other words, because there are significant and complex challenges in the urban environment, leaders must be able to demonstrate strong participatory management qualities aimed at empowering the stakeholders.

Communication in the urban school environment is similar to that in any other school organization. However, there are some major differences. Much of the difference in urban-school communication centers around the multiple constituents that an urban school serves as well as the high level of unemployment, low-skill jobs, poor housing, and other socioeconomic challenges that confront the school's community. When organizing a community-relations strategy for urban schools, leaders should keep in mind several factors identified by Katz and Kahn (1978) such as the following: (a) size of the loop (organization), (b) the transmission process, (c) feedback capacity, (d) efficiency standards and expectations, and (e) the comfort or fit of the network or organization to the expectations and goals of the individuals involved.

Regardless of the common educational goals that urban, suburban, and rural schools share, urban schools are different. The ethnic and diverse populations that typically constitute large percentages of the urban school's student body create a substantial difference in the urban school when compared to the populations of schools in other communities. The diverse populations in urban schools require unique public-relations strategies. Wiedmer (1996) has identified the following characteristics of the public-relations programs in urban districts. Urban school districts consistently refer to the following:

- Significant curricular changes to include issues of global economy to infuse technology, and to cover environmental concerns
- Reform efforts incorporating site-based management, local school councils, and democratic decision-making
- Multicultural and interracial education
- Student discipline related to gang violence
- Bilingual education, special education, gifted and talented education, vocational education, and tech prep
- School dropout rates and dropout prevention programs
- Safe communities and urban renewal programs
- Magnet and alternative schools
- Busing and transportation programs

- ◆ Programs for at-risk and disadvantaged students
- ◆ Master plans to improve the physical environment, community relations, school attendance, and academic performance

These are issues that confront all urban school districts. By coordinating an effective communication plan, school leaders can more easily coordinate their efforts aimed at assisting students to become successful.

THE RELATIONSHIP MODEL: HOME, SCHOOL, AND COMMUNITY INTERACTION

Research results have been consistent in terms of identifying a holistic strategy to improve the overall success of urban schools. For program effectiveness, urban schools must utilize a traditional model of community interaction, namely, the relationship model. The relationship model suggests that a degree of connection must exist between the home, school, and community.

The Milwaukee, Wisconsin, school district has been described as offering "families-based" schools. In other words, the school in the urban community becomes more than just a place open from Monday through Friday and where there is a playground for children. Each school actually becomes a symbolic edifice that brings people of the community together. The relationship model suggests there must be true and equal collaboration between all three constituent entities. As single entities, none of these groups can be successful without the support and collaboration of the other two. Therefore, it becomes important for school leaders to understand that the success of the school organization is contingent upon the nature of the relationship of the home, school, and community. This relationship must be nurtured and supported by trust, collaboration, and responsibility.

As a reflective practitioner, I need to mention that collaboration is not always easy, especially when there are power and political issues that can distract the focus of the organization. Some of the common obstacles limiting effective community relations include the following:

- ◆ Organizational trust
- ◆ Historical and ideological baggage
- ◆ The inability to create a fair and equitable resource allocation system
- ◆ Creditability within the community
- ◆ Bureaucratic complications
- ◆ Political conflict that does not result in a shared vision

When attempting to achieve community interaction on school issues, leaders should be aware that organizational size has a significant impact on the ability to communicate effectively. In large organizations, there is often selective perception of the information presented. For example, bits and pieces of information offered may be filtered by individuals' interests, biases, and values. Also, in urban educational organizations, constituency groups that orchestrate responses to unfavorable or unpopular information may impact school leaders' communication strategy.

A common truism espoused in many management and leadership-training programs is this: "The only way to survive individually is to think and act cooperatively." As we approach the twenty-first century, urban school organizations cannot survive and be successful alone. The schools must act as a cooperative unit or all individuals will fail urban children.

ADDRESSING INTERNAL COMMUNITY RELATIONS

A cohesive, urban community-relations program will make strong efforts to support and encourage those internal stakeholders who are integral to the organization's success. These stakeholders include teachers, students, administrators, cooks, custodians, bus drivers, secretaries, educational assistants, playground attendants, as well as the superintendent. This group includes any other individuals or groups in the school organization who directly and consistently interact with children. These individuals should have a vested interest in the success of urban children. Opportunities for collaboration, integration of ideals and concepts, and continuous improvement and assessment procedures should be encouraged in urban school environments. Because of the multiple cultures, languages, and other pressing social challenges, the appreciation and consideration for these groups are often at odds. Issues such as negotiations, strikes, school-board decision-making, and pupil academic success and behavior take on additional significance because of the size and media focus on the urban community. An effective school community-relations program is at the heart of building a foundation on which an entire school district can stand.

It is perhaps very useful to discuss at this point the term "relationship." The relationship established between the school leadership team and the internal personnel and external public is dynamic. As our personal relationships change and adjust to issues and concerns, so do the relationships that exist between school leadership and internal and external constituents. A relationship requires time, patience, goal-orientation, vision, and a commitment to stay focused on mutually agreed upon objectives.

Addressing External Community Relations

The diverse socioeconomic levels of urban school communities provide enormous challenges to urban school leaders, who make a commitment to a cohesive group of stakeholders. The group that school leaders consider an important internal group (students) ultimately must also be considered as one of the most significant groups that is also a part of the external community. Students can perhaps offer the strongest voice of support in the homes of our community. Students can provide direct information to parents about the success or failure of the school.

This book has devoted attention to the role of parents in urban schools. Without question, parents are one of the most significant external groups that deserve committed energy and time from school leaders. The interesting question developing across the country, however, focuses on those adults who do not have children in the local school district. As the percentage of adults without children in schools increases every year, urban school leaders must cultivate this group and target them for school engagement.

All communities have key spokespersons. These spokespersons are often leaders in the community and interested in the success of their children and the children of their neighbors. In urban communities, prominent roles are given to local business and finance leaders, church officials, and community activists. These people can be both supportive and often vocal about the direction of the school district. Urban school leaders must be articulate and visionary when communicating the specific goals and objectives of the district and all efforts should be made to include as many stakeholders as possible.

The ability to manage and direct external groups requires that school leaders be able to handle conflict and subsequent verbal and media attacks regarding their professional judgment and decision-making. When addressing issues of conflict in urban environments, leaders should be aware of the consequences of words taken out of context, anger directed toward an individual or group, and the ultimate impact of this conflict on children who can typically ill-afford not to take advantage of their education.

THE POLITICAL NATURE OF URBAN SCHOOL COMMUNITIES

Much of the conflict in urban school organizations is grounded in political ideology and personal career planning at the expense of urban children. Politics have often been viewed negatively and many educational organizations are reluctant to be viewed as political participants. However, school leaders quickly recognize that educational decisions are clearly connected with political ideology and social interpretation. At the federal level, the creation of the Department of Education was perhaps the singular symbolic gesture that formalized the political nature of schools and government. The role of state departments of education, in addition to many of the reform reports of the early 1980s, clearly suggested that the interpretation of an elected policymaker could have a tremendous impact on school children.

Urban school communities provide the most enlightening examples of political analysis, because of their size, structure, exposure to media, and the need to respond to multiple interest groups. In addition, it is not uncommon that aspiring politicians use the school board as a stepping-stone to higher political office. The exposure school board members receive from the media and national print media make them likely choices for other political offices.

Politics have been an academic area of investigation in organizations for many years. Much of political dynamics is crafted around power and the ability to control resources. Banner and Gagne (1995) suggested that the resulting action of politics is determined primarily by self-motivation, which may not be in concert with the goals of the organization. It is a common belief in business and education that as resources become less available ambiguity increases, and there is likely an increase in organizational politics.

Another term often used in lieu of politics is influence. Essentially, individuals attempt to assert their influence with others in an organization in order to achieve a desired goal. Yukl and Falbe (1990) have provided some standard definitions regarding tactics used to exert influence. The authors identified (a) pressure tactics, (b) upward appeals, (c) exchange tactics, (d) coalition tactics, (e) ingratiating tactics, (f) rational persuasion, (g) inspirational appeals, and (f) consultation tactics.

In urban school organizations, all of these tactics are used to influence decision-makers, such as administrators, teachers, and school-board members. For example, pressure tactics are often used as political ploys. When influential, key communicators in the community, politicians in city government, or constituents make phone calls to school leaders, this may be viewed as power-players using pressure tactics. All too often, these pressure tactics involve either the support of or opposition to policies, which may result in some negative reaction by the school organizations. Special interest groups use pressure tactics in order to change or to maintain a certain policy or procedure.

Upward appeals occur when a person seeks to persuade or influence a leader's position by conveying that the manager or leader in a higher decision-making position has already approved of the identified request. Upward appeals are interesting, because they involve decisions that could affect the careers of upwardly mobile leaders, who show great concern regarding outcomes of the decisions they attempt to influence. Individuals interested in advancing their careers are always interested in the perception of the issue. Policy analysis and policymaking may be influenced by created perceptions that may not be accurate.

Perhaps the most dangerous form of organizational politics is the exchange tactic. This process essentially suggests that an interested party will make an explicit or implicit promise that another person will receive an identified reward or tangible benefit, if that other person complies with a request or proposal. Of course, once a person has complied, there is the understanding that the favor will be returned. Concepts often referred to as the "old boys club" and the "glass ceiling" depend on the exchange tactic. Another disturbing element with this tactic is that ethical or moral issues may impact the decision-making process.

The coalition tactic is also used considerably in urban school organizations. A person employing the coalition tactic seeks the aid of others to persuade decision-makers to do something or uses the stated support of others as an argument for leaders to agree with a policy or issue. These tactics often gain media attention, because of the vocal nature of the coalition. If there are ethnic, racial, gender, or economic issues at stake, the coalition tactic can bring conflict, ambiguity, and power struggles. Labor tensions in urban school districts provide a prime example of the work of coalitions. In the classic battle between the management and labor, each group attempts to identify allies and supporters who will form effective coalitions in support of their agendas. Coalitions may be more interested in remaining active than in identifying critical issues for urban children.

Leaders experience ingratiating tactics when a person seeks to get the leader in good spirits and to think positively about the petitioner before asking for desired action. When the petitioners use what they perceive to be a logical argument and factual documentation to persuade the leader to support their policy initiative or proposal, the petition is attempting to use rational persuasion. Inspirational appeals happen when a person makes an emotional request that arouses empathy, which may appeal to values and ideals.

Engaging in consultation tactics entails seeking a leader's participation in creating and implementing the proposed strategy or idea. This method comes closest to positive collaboration. In consultation, however, there is not a guaranteed response or action. This perspective allows the most input regarding the benefit for children and the subsequent effects on their growth and development.

Research indicates that politics can lead to a decline in morale and inferior organizational performance. Ultimately politics limits the decision-making and control that employees have in organizations (Voyer, 1994). Researchers, such as Drory (1993), have indicated that politics can become so dominating within organizations that stakeholders lose their view of the primary organizational objective. However, a possibility exists that political interaction provides an opportunity for diverse opinions, which may increase effective communication and decision-making in urban school organizations.

CHARTER SCHOOLS

Charter schools have recently been identified as one of the most serious challenges to the continuation of public education as we know it. When President William Jefferson Clinton provided the opportunity for parents to increase their choice and options for schooling, the charter-school movement received its strongest endorsement. In addition to charter schools, vouchers are also viewed as a key threat to the deterioration of public schools.

Charter schools have become increasingly popular as people attempt to identify a better option than pubic schools. The perception by many parents and civic leaders is that public schools are no longer a viable option for educating children as evidenced by poor discipline, low achievement scores, and lack of academic competitiveness with other nations. More states are examining charter schools as a viable option to traditional public education and are receiving financial support from state legislatures to create these "special schools." Urban schools, in particular, are accused of being ineffective. As a result, charter schools and vouchers are being presented in urban communities as the savior for public education. According to Buechler (1997), "charter schools are independent, results-oriented, publicly funded schools of choice designed to be run by teachers or others who contracted with a public sponsor" (p. 60). These schools are created by a charter or contract with and are sponsored by a local entity such as a university or community association. The sponsoring organization has the authority to revoke the charter, if the policies or guidelines are not achieved.

The primary distinction between a charter school and a "regular" school is the release from traditional guidelines and regulations. This distinction is significant because the question that is often asked is: If a charter school can receive public funds and be released from policies and procedures, then why not release the regular schools of these regulations as well? Charter schools differ in different parts of the country. The first type of charter school is basically independent from the local school organization, such as those found in Minnesota. In Wisconsin, charter schools are created as independent schools, but are extensions of the local school organization (US Charter Schools, 1997).

POLITICAL ISSUES ASSOCIATED WITH CHARTER SCHOOLS

There are political implications for charter schools and vouchers. Four issues surrounding charters schools and voucher programs appear to be controversial and carry potential political ramifications. These issues are (a) the status of special education, (b) local governance and accountability, (c) racial and socioeconomic segregation, and (d) public funding for private ventures.

A question regarding charter schools that has not been sufficiently answered is: What happens to students with disabilities who may not be able to attend a charter school? Are the rights of special-education students being addressed and if not, is this a violation of these students' right to an education? If a child is not "traditional" or "normal," are they excluded from these schools, which are theoretically designed to improve the educational process as well as achievement?

Perhaps the most significant question for charter schools is whether funding is available to make the facilities consistent with standards placed into law and applicable to traditional public schools. Also central to this issue is the concern of personnel. Is there an assumption that teachers will be able to meet the needs of special-education students without any special training or skills development? Or will the charter school simply be permitted to experiment with children as test cases? If accountability standards are consistent with public schools, then the need for charter schools is questionable. The primary premise for the creation of charter schools was to eliminate the counterproductive regulations and paperwork. The issue of offering special education may actually produce the outcomes charter schools were created to avoid.

The local governance and accountability of education has been the hallmark of American education. Because most charter schools are not governed by elected school policymakers (boards of education), there is limited supervision, evaluation, and accountability that can be employed by the citizens of the community. As with many new projects, charter schools may be enjoying the benefits of the "halo effect." Simply put, the attention provided to charter schools because they are so new, controversial, and innovative, may increase the success of these schools. The reality may be that there are no actual differences in the schools when compared to traditional public schools.

One of the challenges for urban schools organizations in terms of charter schools and vouchers focuses on the issue of segregation. For example, in Hilton Head, South Carolina, racial issues surfaced when there was a proposal for a charter school in the district. Concerns were raised when the local board of education refused to grant a charter because they feared it would promote segregation by providing a school alternative to non-minority students. The current racial composition in the district was fifty percent African-American and fifty percent white (Charter Schools, 1997). Given the history of racial tension caused by school decision-making, legislators are not eager to be perceived as recreating a segregated school system using public dollars.

The fourth and perhaps most significant challenge to charter schools is the issue of public funds and allocation of resources. At a time when most public schools are struggling to meet financial obligations, there are tax dollars being spent on schools that may be segregated at best and at worst controversial. Since the late 1970s, American conservatives have demanded there be no new taxes. Consequently, local taxpayers are concerned that public schools are spending even more public funds for charter schools.

SUMMARY

Community relations and politics are central to the success of any school organization. Urban schools and communities need to be able to redesign and restructure efforts to meet the prevailing political challenges. Urban school leaders must be knowledgeable about the future of the district. This means communicating with their internal and external publics as well as maintaining and expanding political resources that assist in decision-making in the best interest of urban children.

Charter schools and vouchers continue to be controversial throughout the nation. In urban school communities, the fight between charter schools and traditional public schools takes on additional pressure because there is a common belief in the inner-city that charter schools and voucher programs will simply take away the successful students who are currently enrolled in city schools. What may remain will be the "academic leftovers"—students who, for whatever reason, were unable to get out of their current school into a specialized school. Based on the realities politics and power, those students and families most likely to be "left behind" are those who are least powerful, least influential, and those who hold limited political and economic resources.

9

CREATING CHANGE IN URBAN SCHOOLS

INTRODUCTION

The prevailing impression many Americans hold regarding the urban school environment is one of a massive bureaucracy crippled by its own size, inefficiency, and ineffectiveness. Educational leaders in urban schools are, to a large extent, perceived as being unable to play a significant role in school change and effectiveness because of district size, management diversification, legislative oversight, limited economic resources, issues associated with changing student clientele, competency issues regarding school personnel, and infrastructure demands. Urban school leaders have also been portrayed as being unassertive and reactive concerning school leadership and fiscal management. Academic standards, accountability, and community challenges are issues that are exacerbated by a difficult economy that cripples most school districts, and disproportionately affects urban schools.

Urban school leaders are looking for management techniques to address all of these critical demands. Many of these "new" strategies or trends in educational leadership are repackaged, ineffective tools rather than concrete, workable principles that can be used to implement positive change in urban school communities. This chapter addresses the perceived rhetoric of the post-bureaucratic school in the postmodern era. Key to this topic is this question: "Is there a need for critical analysis of post-bureaucracy and postmodernism concepts in urban school management or are there more pressing educational and social issues that urban school leaders should address?" This chapter also attempts to address the following question: "Are topics such as post-bureaucracy and postmodernism significant enough to warrant discussion from urban school leaders?" What will be the impact of a post-bureaucratic management approach for urban schools in the next century? The chapter also analyzes power and decision-making strategies of urban school leaders and post-bureaucratic challenges to stability and vision in the urban school environment. Recommendations to education-administration programs and school practitioners regarding the importance of understanding the role and mission of the post-bureaucratic urban school leader will also been discussed.

An assessment of today's urban schools typically results in a spectrum of responses by educators. At one end of the spectrum, educators describe urban schools that are in the midst of restructuring, reinvention, and actively participating in organizational change (Cuban, 1970; Edmonds, 1979; Fullan, 1993; Jackson May and Sanders, 1996; Johnson, 1995; Lezotte, 1994; Sanders, 1992; Sanders and Jackson May 1997; Sanders and Reed, 1995). The visionary, proactive view of urban schools would create an educational bureaucracy that is no longer structured and rigid, but that allows organizational decision-making and communication occur with consensus building and broad participation. At the other end of the spectrum— and perhaps the version most believable—it is suggested that urban educational organizations are in chaos and that cities are in social, economic, and political ruin. Heckscher and Donnellon (1994) have offered an ideal organizational model identified as post-bureaucratic which "starts from the master concept that everyone takes responsibility for the success of the whole rather than for a particular job" (p. 15). The post-bureaucratic model of urban education attempts to eliminate organizational barriers to effective and efficient management. This chapter offers some analysis of the role and mission of post-bureaucratic philosophy as it applies to urban educational organizations and leaders. In addition to the analysis, this chapter examines Heckscher's and Donnellon's post-bureaucracy approach for an ideal organizational environment as either rhetoric-oriented or reality-based, and offers recommendations to education-administration programs interested in working with urban schools.

POSTMODERNISM AND POST-BUREAUCRACY

In order to grasp postmodernism and post-bureaucracy, it is critical to review what scholars refer to as the modern period. The modern period has been described as a time when organizational behavior was dominated and controlled by traditional methods of inquiry (Owens, 1995). In traditional methods of inquiry, the laboratory was structured, organized, and all behaviors were expected to be studied and explained logically and sequentially. School organizations, like many other institutions, were studied and examined in similar fashion. Postmodernism (often referred to as post-bureaucratic, poststructuralist, postpositivist, and postanalytic) essentially suggests that ideals, values, beliefs, and assumptions are central to understanding why people in organizations behave the way they do. Owens (1995) noted that:

> the behavior of people at work in educational organizations—individually as well as group—is not merely a reflection of their idiosyncratic personalities but is influenced, if not defined, by the social norms and expectations of the culture that prevail in the organization (p. 6).

Essentially, Owens suggested that in order to understand organizations and the behaviors of people who are employed in them, one must go beyond the structured or bureaucratic formality that exists in most organizations. In order to grasp a valuable and realistic view of school behavior, researchers must develop a postmodern or post-bureaucratic view.

It is important to note from the outset that Heckscher and Donnellon (1994) identified the post-bureaucratic school as an "ideal" organizational concept that does not exist as a working model. The model does not provide examples of organizations for review and analysis that most resemble this "ideal." However, the conceptual model aggressively addresses several growing concerns among organizational leaders, such as organizational change and chaos without goals, missions, direction for members, in addition to a growing concern for school clients and the community at large.

Richard Edwards, in his 1979 book, *Contested Terrain: The Transformation of the Workplace in the Twentieth Century*, outlined a transformational workplace and questioned the existence of traditional hierarchical organizations. Edwards (1979) noted that organizations once marked by unconstrained managerial power and characterized by impersonality and intolerance were moving in a direction where workers would contribute and participate in organizational decision-making to a larger extent than at any other time in the twentieth century.

In the educational arena, and particularly in urban school environments, organizational change has been comprehensive, complex, and difficult to manage. This difficulty in management and the issue of impersonality and intolerance of school organizations require school leaders to seek effective techniques for managing urban school bureaucracies and thereby urban children. Researchers have known for some time about the organizational problems faced by urban school environments and the implications for at-risk children (Ravitch, 1983; Sanders, 1992; Sanders and Reed, 1995; Taylor, 1989; Willie, 1985).

Urban school organizations have attempted to identify effective strategies to manage facilities, children, financial dilemmas, as well as the changing demographic variables in the immediate and global communities. Irvine (1990) suggested that urban school organizations would need to respond to the crisis concerning African-American children. Irvine noted that when African-American children are compared to European-American children, African-American children are two to four times as likely to be poor and live in substandard housing with an unemployed teenage mother. The urban educational organization and school leaders have to consider being responsive to single parenthood, family and community transformation, as well as the results of inadequate prenatal or postnatal health-care (Irvine, 1990). Furthermore, the recent trend of violence and crime, in all geographic areas, and particularly in economically depressed communities, suggest that educational organizations and bureaucracies need to address the way in which they have traditionally managed schools. At the very least, these social issues point to that fact that schools are part of the collaborative answer for stakeholders seeking significant change. Urban educational bureaucracies have been under tremendous social, economic, and political pressure. Urban school leaders have been compelled to address numerous issues: socioeconomic forces, political bargaining, organizational decision-making, bilingual education, discipline, social-class prejudice, substance abuse, teacher competence, and student achievement (Comer, 1997; Kantor and Brenzel, 1992; Lomotey, 1990; Sanders, 1996). Continued investigation of the post-bureaucratic school organization indicates that the approach is either rhetoric-oriented or reality-based.

MAJOR COMPONENTS OF THE POST-BUREAUCRATIC SCHOOL

The post-bureaucratic ideal model has received attention in recent years due to the lack of success and achievement of traditional bureaucratic organizations. Heckscher and Donnellon (1994) have identified a shift from the traditional organizational format to a new consensus-based approach to managing people. The authors delineated twelve general, conceptual positions of the post-bureaucracy model:

- The post-bureaucratic organization builds consensus through institutional dialogue as opposed to "acquiescence to authority, rules, or traditions" (p. 25).

- "Dialogue is defined by the use of influence rather than power" (p. 25). Heckscher and Donnellon suggested that leaders will need to use their influence to direct the organizations and not simply command action. The authors also indicated that "the ability to persuade is based on a number factors, including knowledge of the issue, commitment to shared goals, and proven past effectiveness" (p. 25).

♦ Influence is established upon trust and the post-bureaucratic ideal model is based primarily upon consensus-building and the belief that individual members will benefit from the success of the whole. Heckscher and Donnellon pointed to an organization's ability to implement trust as a critical variable to success. Influence must be based on interdependence whereas, performance is based on all members' productivity and efficiency.

♦ The post-bureaucratic ideal model relies heavily on the organizational mission. This organizational notion resists the traditional belief of values-oriented ideals and focuses instead on "what the company actually seeks to achieve" (p. 25). Heckscher and Donnellon pointed out that "the mission plays a crucial integrating role in an organization that relies less heavily on job definition and rules. Employees need to understand the key objectives in depth in order to coordinate their actions intelligently" (p. 25).

♦ The post-bureaucratic organization must "link individual contributions to the mission," which results in the dissemination of information and company strategy to employees at all levels in the organization. Heckscher and Donnellon indicated that this is important due to the fact that the linking of information allows employees to relate directly their jobs or performance to the mission of the organization. "This enables individuals to break free of boundaries of their defined jobs and to think creatively and cooperatively about improvement in performance" (p. 26). This open information, which is made more accessible by computer technology, flows top-down and is evaluated and critiqued from the bottom up.

♦ "The focus for mission is supplemented by guidelines for action: these, however, take the form of principles rather than rules" (p. 26). The post-bureaucratic model distinguishes between principles and rules and suggests "principles are more abstract, expressing the reasons behind the rules that are typical of bureaucracy" (p. 26). The model illustrates a further advantage of introducing guiding principles rather than enforcing rules: following principles allows for flexibility and intelligent interaction in the transitional environment. However, flexibility can be abused, which can directly threaten an organization's effectiveness. Potential ineffectiveness is less likely when leaders trust team members to follow principles and schedule reviews or evaluations of the effectiveness of principles.

♦ Post-bureaucratic organizations must frequently reconstruct their decision-making strategies. Decision-making strategies in post-bureaucratic organizations typically implement "meta-decision making" mechanisms. By this Heckscher and Donnellon (1994) indicated that "meta-decision making" occurs in organizations that implement cross-functional and cross-level committees or teams that handle decision-making and develop appropriate principles.

♦ A key variable in post-bureaucracy ideology is the nature of relationships and community. Post-bureaucratic relationships are formalized and specialized. "It is a matter of knowing who to go to for a particular problem or issue, rather than a matter of building a stable network of friendship relations" (p. 27). Parsons (1969) stated "influence relations are wider and more diverse, but also shallower and more specific, than those of traditional community" (p. 536).

♦ Post-bureaucratic organizations have "open processes of association and peer evaluation, so that people get a relatively detailed view of each others' strengths and weaknesses" (Heckscher and Donnellon, 1994, p. 27).

♦ Heckscher and Donnellon (1994) described open-oriented post-bureaucratic organizations as demonstrating intercorrelational concepts on career aspirations and the importance of working with other constituencies within the organization. The authors believe that post-bureaucratic organizations rely heavily on employees entering and leaving the organization; employees reject the traditional notion of "going it alone" for an openness that allows consensus-building among all members of the organization.

♦ Post-bureaucratic organizations respond to equity concerns in two ways: a consensus effort to change rules into principles and an increased need to recognize varied individual performances. The authors acknowledged some difficulty in addressing these two principles in any organization, but recommended "the solution involves the development of public standards of performance, openly discussed and often negotiated with individual employees, against which they will be measured" (p. 28).

♦ Time elements in the post-bureaucratic organization are attached to an expectation of consistent change. The authors believe traditional bureaucracies implement standard cycles of review under specific time frames. In the post-bureaucratic model, because change is constant, the organization uses time-oriented reviews based on the nature of the specific organizational objective and not necessarily because the calendar requires a review session. "The time periods are not necessarily keyed to the annual budget cycle: They may be shorter or longer, depending on the nature of the task. This flexibility of time is essential to adaptiveness because the perception of a problem depends on putting it in the right time frame" (p. 28).

ROLE AND MISSION OF THE URBAN SCHOOL LEADER

A review of Heckscher's and Donnellon's twelve basic components of post-bureaucracy offers an opportunity to analyze the overall theory and to specifically determine the effectiveness of such a system in urban educational environments. One major assumption Heckscher and Donnellon (1994) make is that schools should be operated like "new" companies. These "new" companies or organizations place emphasis on consensus-building, teamwork, and a comprehensive focus on organizational effectiveness. There are at least two central themes that must be addressed if a post-bureaucratic model can be implemented in urban schools. Urban school leaders should be particularly interested in the role and mission of power and decision-making in a post-bureaucratic organization.

POWER ISSUES IN THE URBAN ORGANIZATION

Heckscher and Donnellon's (1994) notion of *gemeinschaft* clearly suggests a basic battleground exists for power in any organization. *Gemeinschaft* suggests there is a battle or friction between an individual's beliefs and values in institutional commitment that conflict with individual autonomy. Because all organizations seek to determine their unique focus or role in a complex modern society, this conflict becomes the battleground for power in the organization. Because urban school organizations are large and complex, there are battles for power. Whether individuals seek commitment to institutional values and norms or whether they remain closely associated with individual autonomy will likely determine how he or she will use power. Obviously, it would be ideal for power to be vested in people who are strongly committed to the institution. Unfortunately, in a number of urban schools, it appears that the individuals with power are more interested in what the organization can do for them than in what they can do for the school organization.

Earlier chapters have discussed a number of problems associated with urban schools. Not only are the problems massive, difficult, and seemingly impossible to resolve, but they also appear to arise from many areas. In other words, the difficulties urban school administrators and leaders face derive from a number of sources: politics, society, economics, and community. Difficulties also arise from differing values and moral dilemmas. The interplay of the challenges and the sources from which they arise create difficulty in prioritizing problems as despair mounts among the organization members. If an individual in power is more concerned with individual aims than with institutional issues, it becomes difficult to move organizations in a progressive direction.

Urban-school bureaucracies typically operate on structured rules and regulations. These rules and regulations have been used predominately in urban schools because of organizational magnitude and human complexity within the organization. However, within these rules and regulations, aspects of traditional power— whether held by reason of position, knowledge, or coercion—have been yielded to and managed by bureaucrats. A post-bureaucratic approach calls for rules to be eliminated and replaced with principles. Furthermore, these principles are directly correlated to the mission of the organization. Heckscher and Donnellon (1994) noted that the advantages of having principles are flexibility and the opportunity to allow intelligent responses from all members of the organization. Unfortunately, flexibility can be counterproductive when members intentionally or unintentionally abuse the organization's flexibility. Although Heckscher and Donnellon prescribed a technique to reduce this abuse (trust and periodic review of principles), it is unclear whether this component of post-bureaucracy is adaptable to the urban school bureaucracy.

The role of power with regard to influence is important in urban school bureaucracies. Post-bureaucratic organizations replace traditional bureaucratic power with influence. Obviously, with influence comes the ability to persuade. Influence, in the post-bureaucratic organization, is not based on official position or title. Traditional bureaucratic responses based on punitive or coercive power held by a superior are reduced. Heckscher and Donnellon noted, "the influence of hierarchy is not embedded in permanent offices, and is to a far greater degree than bureaucracy based on the consent of, and the perception of, other members in the organization" (p. 25). Therefore, power is reduced or eliminated and replaced with trust, influence, and persuasion.

In school organizations, positions are typically associated with competence and knowledge. In a traditional bureaucracy one would expect a person in a highly responsible, visible position to demonstrate knowledge, commitment, and competence. If urban school organizations adopted a post-bureaucratic philosophy, the traditional use of power and chain-of-command would need to be addressed. Although many urban school systems have adopted forms of site-based management and total quality management, the acceptance of a post-bureaucratic approach would likely challenge the very foundation on which the traditional bureaucracies has been built. The post-bureaucratic model would usher in a new approach to urban school management. Implementing the post-bureaucratic model would likely introduce major shifts in power. Critics of post-bureaucracies indicate that this approach leads to some degree of continued chaos; however, others praise the formative, positive changes in the organization.

In summary, the role of power in post-bureaucratic organizations places emphasis on influence, persuasion, shared goals, and proven past effectiveness. The implementation of a post-bureaucratic model in urban school organizations would require a total shift in current policy and procedures. The shift to a post-bureaucratic model of management would cause much concern at every level in the traditional school bureaucracy. Some of these concerns include job security, pay scales, binding contractual agreements, financial support, and commitment levels and involvement of teachers, nonteaching personnel, and the community.

DECISION-MAKING ISSUES IN URBAN ORGANIZATIONS

The second major variable is the process by which decisions are made in post-bureaucratic organizations. This discussion can be divided into four areas of concern: (a) the role of institutional dialogue, (b) institutional dialogue and the attachment to "influence," (c) decision-making methods, and (d) the time dedicated to decision-making.

Post-bureaucratic organizations emphasize institutional dialogue, which typically entails allowing employees to interact with each other in a collegial manner as they make decisions. Heckscher and Donnellon credit institutional dialogue to Haberman's (1991) concept of "ideal speech." Ideal speech in organizations is an open-ended communication process where all members have complete authority to verbalize their positions on any issue without threat of loss of employment or punitive actions by traditional managing decision-makers. Leaders, who usually make management decisions autonomously and summarily and exclude the input of those assigned to do the work, may be uncomfortable with this approach. Remember, however, that "ideal speech" is based on the foundation that all individuals have a high level of institutional commitment.

A second variable in decision-making encompasses institutional dialogue and the attachment to "influence." Ideally, if some people in the organization are more persuasive than others, attachment to influence allows each individual to state a position and allows members to determine direction. Traditional, "official" position would not be a factor in decision-making. This influence approach would create an open environment for those who have strong communication and articulation skills. Heckscher and Donnellon (1994) believe that influence is based on several factors, including "knowledge of issues, commitment to shared goals, and proven past effectiveness" (p. 25). Of these three factors impacting influence, traditional rank-and-file employees would be able to adopt shared goals immediately. The other two areas—"knowledge of issues" and "proven past effectiveness"—would require traditional managers to surrender valuable information to the same individuals with whom, in essence, managers would be in direct "competition." Initially, surrendering information might seem unlikely; however, when traditional managers and employees share a decision that benefits the organization, the results of the decision benefit all involved members—including the manager "responsible" for the decision.

Heckscher and Donnellon (1994) describe a third facet of organizational collaboration: "meta-decision making strategy." Meta-decision making demands that all members in an organization participate in decision-making. This community approach to decision-making allows for consensus-building, institutional dialogue, and open boundaries.

Trust is another determining quality that urban school leaders must consider as they adopt a post-bureaucratic strategy. Bureaucracies, by their nature, are departmentalized. Those who work in large bureaucracies realize that one side of the building may not know or care what the other side is doing; there is a strong need to assure that each specialized compartment is perceived as important and necessary to bureaucratic decision-makers. In essence, urban school leaders may be perceived as distrusting of each other and ultimately more concerned with proving their own worth (individual autonomy) and not as concerned about the productivity and efficiency of the entire organization (institutional commitment). This distrust in school organizations is inherent in a traditional bureaucracy. Therefore making the transition to a post-bureaucratic organization requires a total overhaul of central office and middle management. It also demands a total commitment to the essence of post-bureaucracy by teachers, administrators, and all invested members of the school organization.

A final aspect of decision-making is time. The post-bureaucratic organization essentially eliminates the notion of annual review. This new management style marks time and specified periods on the basis of the task being accomplished. Heckscher and Donnellon (1994) believe "the ability to manage varying time frames is a major advantage of the post-bureaucratic system" (p. 28). For decision-making in the urban school organization to be effective, flexible time frames could create instability, if employees are not knowledgeable or confident about the longevity of a decision. However, the new strategy allows employees the authority to revisit and reevaluate principles simply by bringing an issue forward for discussion.

The implementation of a post-bureaucratic model would require a complete reorganization of most urban school organizations. This model places emphasis on consensus-building, team problem-solving, and a conceptual view of relationships regarding matters internal and external to the organization. Essentially, power in post-bureaucratic organizations depends largely upon trust, interdependence, and the elimination of traditional management authority. Decision-making in this model requires consensus through institutional dialogue, which is affected by influence. Each individual becomes a decision-maker, essentially creating a type of meta-decision making organization. Lastly, time constraints and components in decision-making do not exist and all decisions are never permanent.

The ideal model of post-bureaucracy is fascinating as well as complicated. Can the model be implemented in fact? The model is either rhetoric-oriented or reality-based. The question often asked by superintendents and principals is this: "What does this mean to me in my everyday job?" In other words, is this approach something that will make my job easier or better? The answer is, "yes." These questions quickly cause stakeholders to suggest there is a role and mission for the urban school leader in a post-bureaucratic model. However, the extent of the role and mission is contingent upon the degree of collaboration that occurs throughout the entire system. Some examination is required to determine whether this model is merely theory from the "ivory tower" or whether urban school leaders can make the model reality.

RHETORIC OR REALITY

One of the major responsibilities for those working in educational programs is to bridge theoretical concepts with practical applications. School leaders, and especially professors, have often been accused of using a rhetoric-oriented, reactionary approach to resolving school problems. This reported rhetoric is typically seen as grounded in unrealistic, abstract, and unachievable policies and programs. In other words, when exploring theoretical ideologies such as post-bureaucracy, it is critical to be able to determine whether the concept is practical and applicable to schools.

At first glance, it might appear that post-bureaucratic leadership is another unrealistic model not unlike models already proposed as a panacea for schools. The notion that post-bureaucracy is rhetoric-oriented means that these ideas are so "out of touch" with the "real school world" that implementing the model would lead to major disruptions in the urban school organization.

Conversely, post-bureaucracy could be perceived as a reality-based philosophy with merit. It could be viewed as the only answer to address the perceived or actual mediocrity in urban school organizations. The following description analyzes the opposing perspectives.

THE RHETORIC PERSPECTIVE

Because so many of the quick-fix answers for urban schools appear to be rhetoric, it would seem reasonable to be suspect of a post-bureaucratic form of leadership for school organizations. Thus, this form of leadership has met initially with severe criticism, as is often true any new idea. One of the major criticisms of post-bureaucracy is the increase in the number of decision-makers. This argument would suggest that an increase would lead to additional procedures, policies, programs and rules. In a pure post-bureaucratic organization, where consensus-building is sought and received, the sheer ability of the organization to handle all of the input will require more rules and procedures. While attempting to reduce or eliminate bureaucratic red tape, a possibility might be an actual increase in bureaucratic interaction and further the difficulty of resolving complex issues in large school systems. More decision-makers could equal more discussion, more debate, and more time on organizational tasks with fewer results.

A second criticism of post-bureaucracy as rhetoric pertains to the elimination of lines of authority and levels of responsibility. Critics indicate that the elimination of these lines might lead to organizational chaos. By discouraging compartmentalization, post-bureaucratic organizations could lead to an even larger bureaucracy. This greater bureaucracy would be hampered by duplication of effort, reviews of standard policies at the request of dissatisfied employees, and additional time to establish consensus. Interdependence and learning curves of employees with limited experience in participating in technical or global decision-making would further hamstring the bureaucracy. In addition to these concerns, the post-bureaucratic organization would need to consistently maintain procedures to eliminate self-centered individuals and power-brokering.

Another perception of post-bureaucracies is that the organization would have too many leaders, and be leaderless at the same time. In other words, the post-bureaucratic organization would have a number of decision-makers, but no individual or group would be responsible for decisions and policies after they had been implemented. This issue focuses on responsibility and accountability. Group decision-making allows individuals not totally committed to the vision (or plan of direction) an opportunity for disassociation and disloyalty without feeling any responsibility or accountability for their actions or the agreed-upon decisions of the group. Other related concerns are policies establishing majority rule and the establishment of organizational subcultures. Majority-rule policies are effective when there is a sufficient majority that agrees with the planned policy. For example, if a vote on a major policy issue is taken and a policy is approved by a fifty-one to forty-nine percent majority, it is reasonable to conclude that a considerable number of employees might believe so strongly in their position that securing a total commitment for implementing the policy would be difficult, if not impossible. Also, the forty-nine percent minority could evolve into an organizational subculture that could destroy any consensus-building or teamwork plans.

THE REALITY PERSPECTIVE

The reality perspective of the post-bureaucratic discussion directs our attention to developing a new and innovative approach to problem-solving in urban school organizations. While there have been ideas, programs, and strategies recommended for urban schools, most seem to address only a portion of the multifaceted problems faced by these organizations. Consistent and effective change in urban organizations must occur on the level where decisions and policies are created, initiated, and implemented. In essence, the organizational power and decision-making foundation must be impacted in such a way that the entire organization changes at the same time and in the same way. Traditional decision-making, power, communication patterns, and other forms of interaction in bureaucracies would need to have a complete organizational overhaul, and this clearly means change.

Creating a post-bureaucratic urban school organization would require current administrators, teachers, students, parents, community organizations, and the business sector to "reinvest" in urban schools. While the idea of coordinating all of these groups, developing a mission, and building consensus would be difficult and demanding, it would require all segments of these populations to come to the inevitable conclusion that if this coordination and collaboration does not occur, urban schools will be relegated to mediocrity, meager existences, and second-class educational citizenship.

The creation of a post-bureaucratic system would mean interdependence. In traditional organizations independence has been valued and evaluated by rules and procedures. Decision-making has been power based. The conditions facing metropolitan schools and communities are interrelated and in order to implement long-range planning, the answers must also be interrelated. Therefore, urban schools would need to eliminate traditional bureaucracies and create a new "post-urban" school.

A POST-URBAN SCHOOL ORGANIZATION

Schools do not operate in a vacuum or independently. A post-urban school organization would adopt principles such as institutional dialogue, missions that reflect the dreams and hopes of the entire organization, trust, and consensus-building policies. Merely because no post-bureaucratic organization currently exists does not mean that urban school organizations should not attempt to make this philosophy a reality. A post-urban school would adopt qualities and characteristics of a "full-service school" or a school operated according to participatory management. These approaches require regular and significant employee involvement in organizational decision-making. For example, post-urban school employees would set goals, resolve problems, make decisions, establish and enforce performance goals, as well as establish principles for keeping the organization on target with respect to goals, objectives, and mission. Contemporary organizational life can be complex. Success of a post-urban school would require shared decision-making and variable power and responsibility.

One of the questions critics typically ask is this: What happens to the traditional administrator in a post-urban school organization? In the post-urban school environment, the administrator becomes a leader among leaders. The administrator takes on the role of facilitator, confidant, and communicator. This newly devised role for the administrator requires a reevaluation of current job descriptions and requires both teachers and administrators to have their merit and salary increases correlated to the success of the children in their building. Since schools are ultimately judged and evaluated on the basis of student achievement, what better way to build investment in the school community than by building it as a team.

CONCLUSIONS AND RECOMMENDATIONS

As school leaders prepare for the twenty-first century, the need to examine effective techniques for managing a transitional clientele becomes one of the most critical components of change. The questions that remain for school leaders include the following:

♦ What change should be made?

♦ Who will be affected by this change?

♦ What will happen to the traditional hierarchical models currently in place and how can all interested stakeholders adopt a post-urban philosophy toward change?

It is clear that change and transition in urban education is inevitable. Urban school leaders must put themselves in a position to direct and guide this change. One positive step urban leaders can take is to examine and implement a post-bureaucratic or post-urban school-leadership model in their districts. This implementation would incorporate strategies such as consensus-building, team-building, meta-decision making, institutional dialogue, influence, and shared power. Many districts have embraced most of, or in some cases the majority of, these principles. The key is directing all action toward the goals and aspirations of the institution. The post-urban school requires a comprehensive overhaul of the hierarchical bureaucracy. This overhaul would require at least two major shifts: one for managers, leaders, and directors and one for traditional rank-and-file employees. Managers would need to relinquish traditional power and control that hierarchical organizations have historically maintained over employees. Traditional employees would need to assume a greater role in and responsibility for the mission, goals, and objectives of the organization. These two major shifts in power and decision-making would create the participatory model necessary for change.

All members of the urban community will be impacted by change. Post-urban school change will involve every family, neighborhood, community, school, and civic organization. All members of the community must join forces for the common good of young urban children, and especially African-American males, who will not succeed unless there is a concerted effort toward holistic change. School leaders must participate as visionaries and proactive facilitators of change.

RECOMMENDATIONS

What are the central themes of change and progress in urban education? There are at least four significant variables that must be attended to, if progress is to be made in urban school organizations. The first consideration should focus on responsibility. Educators, parents, community members, and business and industry must share in the responsibility of rebuilding urban education. No single institution can rebuild urban schools. If we fail to successfully rebuild urban education we will have failed to be responsible to young urban children.

A second consideration is the importance of adjusting personalities and acceptance of urban children. One of the most discouraging aspects of working with urban professionals is the negative attitudes displayed by many of those working with urban children. The job is difficult and there are days that are indeed discouraging. We should be most concerned about those individuals in urban education who have negative feelings toward urban children which are manifested by their low expectation and poor planning with regard to instructional leadership in the classroom. We must accept urban children as they come to us and then we must address issues in their lives that prevent them from being successful.

The third consideration is confronting the concept of an "ideal" school. This chapter supported the position that merely because no ideal school or organization exists does not mean we should not strive to establish the post-urban school. Urban school stakeholders must determine the barriers to creativity and the elements preventing them from being an ideal organization and collaborate with individuals who can assist in making the educational environment much more conducive for learning, success, and effectiveness.

A fourth consideration focuses on believing our dreams for the post-urban school can become a reality. Urban problems cannot be confronted and solved solely by dreams. However, the beginning of the solutions require us to dream and imagine results and then make our dream a reality. Every great solution to any problem began with someone who dared to dream its possibility. Time must be provided for brainstorming about the possibilities for creating the post-urban school.

One of the major goals of this chapter is to provide some recommendations to educational and institutional preparatory programs that want to implement strategies of post-bureaucracy for new and continuing administrators and teachers. The following is a list of recommendations:

- ◆ As public schools undergo systemic transitions, so should institutions of higher education. Educational administration and teacher preparation programs should reexamine curriculum standards and requirements to determine the existence of a contemporary view of educational management, theory, and practice. If a post-bureaucratic or post-urban perspective is not being offered, steps should be taken either to instill the approach into existing curriculum or to create prerequisite courses that specifically address this concern.

- ◆ Educational administration and teacher education programs should begin to teach organizational values that correlate with organizational change. Organizational values would include ideology such as diversity, multiculturalism, administrative inclusion, teacher empowerment, curriculum and instructional development, organizational restructuring, and community involvement. Organizational change would be taught as a means of addressing contemporary educational concerns and require prospective administrators to engage in realistic problem-solving.

♦ Educational administration and teacher education programs should "actively" engage in research of problem areas with practicing administrators, teachers, students, and community members. This "active" engagement would require prospective teachers, administrators, and counselors to respond to real issues in assignments, projects, and requirements. Graduate students would have the opportunity to respond to concerns that are realistic and be able to directly apply new knowledge to current school dilemmas.

♦ Educational administration and teacher education programs must establish or reestablish ties with community agencies and organizations that have some "stake" in the school development. Typically, educational administration programs have been viewed as "ivory towers" or havens for those individuals who have been faithful members of the "old boys' club." In essence, university programs must also become post-bureaucratic, postmodern, and post-urban, if they are going to assist schools in reorganization for the twenty-first century. School practicums or internships must be inclusive and involve organizations with direct and indirect interaction with schools.

♦ Educational administration and teacher education programs must engage at least two key groups in establishing a post-bureaucratic perspective, namely practicing administrators and teachers. Practicing administrators and teachers must have institutional dialogue with leaders of preparation programs in order to create a shared mission and meta-decision making designed to improve the urban school organization. Educational administration programs can be helpful in creating a climate for exchange and establishing rapport. The university is an ideal site to serve as an institutional communication vehicle.

♦ Post-bureaucratic organizations, including educational administration and teacher preparation programs, must become involved in an interdisciplinary approach to problem-solving in schools. Educational administration programs could easily join departments of sociology, science, math, history, communications, and others, in a postmodern attempt to address school problems..

SUMMARY

In summary, it is important to keep in mind that the central ingredient to creating a post-urban school environment is the relationship that exists between professionals. Relationships that are grounded in uncompromising policy and power-based decision-making will not lead to the improvement of urban schools. Ideas and concepts that focus on individualism must be replaced by group and collaborative work. The survival and success of urban schools centers on people who are willing to take calculated risks for the benefit of urban children. Rewards and behaviors that are based on a win-lose philosophy must be replaced with a philosophy of we all win or we all lose.

Again, while there is no ideal organization that exists today, it certainly does not mean we should not attempt to create a system that would encourage participation and consensus-building. Post-bureaucratic perspectives allow educators to dream of organizations that provide missions and roles designed to uplift America's greatest strength, its young people.

10

LEADERSHIP CHALLENGES FOR URBAN SCHOOLS IN THE NEW MILLENNIUM

INTRODUCTION

There are nine summary points that I have drawn from researching and writing this book. The central theme of these points focuses on the importance of serving urban children. This book concludes that within the urban school context, there is a clear need to identify and resolve issues that confront the underrepresented student population. Beyond race, the issue of poverty remains the most injurious element to children in urban schools. The effects of poverty are not visible to the common observer because children in urban schools may not look as though they are suffering from the effects of poverty. However, on closer inspection, it is obvious to educational leaders that children from urban schools need to have hope and inspiration. I contend that children of poverty can achieve hope and inspiration with the help of those who work in urban school communities.

One perspective that became very clear in writing this book is that individuals who work in urban school communities need to seek productive and positive ways to work with children, ways that are meaningful, creative, and that demonstrate a genuine caring attitude about people. In many cases, this means school personnel should learn to treat urban parents and students with respect and sincerity. There is nothing worse than being ignored in a society that sends you daily messages that you are not welcomed or appreciated as a human being. The school becomes the beacon of light in many urban communities and the nature of the interaction between school employees and community members is critical.

The message I intend to send is that urban schools, like most other schools, do not operate in a vacuum and therefore must interact with other entities and institutions that make up the communities they serve. The word "community" has been used quite often in educational circles and the meaning could easily be lost. Urban schools must become communities that combine resources, energy, goals, and a commitment to reconfigure the system in such a way that all children benefit.

The summary points I want to share with readers are as follows:

- The need to identify and train effective urban leaders
- The need to conduct more research on the long-term effectiveness of male- and female-immersion schools
- The need for urban schools to separate classes based on gender
- The need to invest in urban children
- The need to conduct meaningful studies on organizational effectiveness in urban schools
- The need to consolidate community programs that seek to accomplish similar objectives
- The need to enhance teacher collaboration
- The need to recruit more male classroom teachers
- The need to continue to discuss race, gender, and cultural appreciation

THE NEED TO IDENTIFY AND TRAIN EFFECTIVE URBAN LEADERS

There is general agreement in educational circles that a shortage of qualified candidates for school-executive positions exists. In recent years teachers have been less interested in moving into administrative positions. Some of this reluctance to accept administrative positions results from unattractive salaries. However, in addition to salary, there are number of other issues that discourage teachers from becoming administrators. These include student discipline, more work days, conflicts with unions, unhappy parents, proficiency testing, poverty concerns, resource allocation, and political challenges. While these reasons are enough to discourage many would-be administrators, there are some who accept the challenge to transform people and institutions. These individuals must be trained and prepared to meet these difficult challenges. Therefore, educational administration programs cannot prepare administrators as they did fifty years ago. Also, school board members, parents, and community activists must use different approaches and strategies to address urban school community issues. In most cases, in order to recruit future leaders to urban educational administrative positions, a concerted effort must be made to explore spiritual leadership skills.

Spiritual leadership means that the professional working in the urban school community must take an "oath" of commitment to work in urban environments. In other words, the individual must possess a "calling" to work with urban children and parents. This calling must be the result of a genuine interest in helping students and a comfort level to adjust to situations that are unpredictable and transitional. The spiritual leader is an individual who has a comprehensive understanding of the children and adults with whom he or she works. The individual also understands and appreciates historical and cultural implications that impact the urban school community.

CONDUCT MORE RESEARCH ON LONG-TERM EFFECTIVENESS OF MALE- AND FEMALE-IMMERSION SCHOOLS

There is a clear need to complete more research on the long-term effects of male- and female-immersion schools. As noted earlier, because the immersion school approach for African-American males is somewhat new, practitioners and scholars must evaluate the programs effectively to determine overall impact on academic achievement. Although there have been a number of legal challenges to the establishment of immersion schools, there is a need to determine whether these schools can boost achievement scores.

African-American males and females are suffering disproportionately in terms of education, prison rates, and access to professional opportunities when compared to their European-American counterparts. There must be an effort to address these challenges or there is a possibility that an entire generation of young children could be lost. The immersion school should be an option that districts continue to investigate. Pilot projects should be started at the elementary, middle-school, and high-school levels. In addition, evaluations should occur that involve practitioners, university personnel, parents, and community members.

THE NEED FOR ALL URBAN SCHOOLS TO SEPARATE CLASSES BASED ON GENDER

Perhaps the most controversial summary point that I will propose is the need for urban schools to create an entire system that separates boys and girls throughout the K-12 process. Having boys and girls in separate classes will be a tremendous benefit to urban school districts. The structure of the classes will allow for more instruction to occur because less interaction will likely occur between boys and girls. This approach may be particularly beneficial for girls. Research indicates that girls tend to participate less in class in the presence of boys. This will allow girls to prosper in areas such as math and science. Both boys and girls will be allowed to flourish and grow in an environment where the opposite sex would not be an obstacle or distraction.

Separating classes would also allow for program extensions and subject-specific materials to be discussed in class. For males and females, specific areas of focus could include mentoring, rites-of-passage activities and programs, tutorial assistance, group or individual counseling, and a focus on an Afro-centric curriculum. All of these approaches would be beneficial for both boys and girls.

Opponents of this suggestion indicate that it is not natural for boys and girls to be separated and that it violates Title IX. Parochial schools have used separation by gender for years and have met with academic success. Recent court rulings suggest that if there is equality in schools at the contextual level, gender separation could be beneficial for urban school communities.

THE NEED TO INVEST IN URBAN CHILDREN

There is a critical and urgent need to invest in children from urban schools. This investment should result in financial and human resources being channeled directly to urban schools. Many urban facilities are in need of repair and resources are needed for computers and related equipment. The literature documents well the eroding tax base in urban schools and the severe challenges that exist with respect to levies and bond issues. As I suggested earlier, there is a continuing need to focus on those students and families in the urban community.

Gratuitous political dialogue is not beneficial without actual resources to provide for urban children. Political interaction is necessary if urban groups are to experience any substantial change. This investment of resources not only includes various agencies but also administrators, teachers, counselors, parents, and students. There is a strong need for urban parents to take a more active role in school decision-making and hold the urban school and local politicians more responsible for the academic success of their children.

Through community collaboration, parents can learn their roles as active participants in terms of interaction with the school. Research indicates that parents who experienced negative interactions while they were students in school are less likely to interact with school personnel and are less likely to desire to visit the school. While schools must extend themselves, parents must also demonstrate an active role, which enhances and validates the importance of their child's experiences in public education.

Studies on Organizational Effectiveness in Urban Schools

Urban school organizations are complex, bureaucratic, and require a keen understanding of policies and procedures. From an organizational perspective, there is a need for urban schools to restructure themselves in such a way that they are more welcoming and inviting to the general public. It is important that schools change in ways that suggest more significant interaction with children, parents, and the community. Studies on school climate and culture focused exclusively on the urban school are needed. In addition, recommendations for all school personnel should be provided. This book has recommended the creation of a post-urban school community as a philosophical approach. This approach reduces the standard bureaucracy and focuses on team building, trust, influence, and open communication.

Consolidate Community Programs in Urban School Communities

There is a need to consolidate the programs made available for children and adults in the urban community. When programs are consolidated, schools would be have more access to services for children and parents would be able to summarize their activities and programs. Often, there are programs within the community that have the same goal. It would seem logical that this consolidation would maximize resources and ultimately benefit children. Organizations that have a long history of service to the community should mobilize their energies for the common good of urban school children.

Enhance Teacher Collaboration

There is a need for teachers to communicate with each other as well as with related entities within the school. Teachers should be provided time to collaborate during the school day. Teachers should be willing to work with students before and after school. There is also a need for principals and central office administrators to have two-way communication regarding the success or failure of children under their care. School personnel, especially teachers, should not send a message to children that they don't care. The message should be "not only do I care, but I am willing to make a difference."

Recruit More Male Teachers

The need to recruit more male teachers is important in all districts. Male teachers are beneficial for both boys and girls. As I noted earlier, the messages of socialization are sufficiently strong such that the inability to interact with an African-American male teacher could have long term implications. The presence of African-American male teachers would serve as a symbolic gesture that could influence these young people for the rest of their lives. Recruiting teachers of color, and especially African-American teachers, has proven to be a difficult task. The more successful districts not only recruit underrepresented teachers from university campuses but employ non-traditional methods such as training teacher aides in more instructional methods in order to assist the teacher, as well as exploring alternative certification policies for administrators and teachers.

The Importance of Discussing Race, Gender, and Cultural Appreciation

Race, gender, and culture are three areas that typically cause debate, frustration, and anxiety among school personnel. More importantly, for children, a negative experience in childhood can impact the child to a degree that causes inappropriate behavior later in life. Urban schools need to be hospitals where injuries of race, gender, and cultural appreciation can be mended successfully and allow the individual to live free of the pain.

RECOMMENDATIONS FOR PRACTICE FOR URBAN SCHOOL LEADERS

The following is an abbreviated list of recommendations for urban school leaders interested in reflective analysis on community relations and politics and creating effective change in urban school communities.

♦ Urban school leaders must become reflective about their occupations. This requires the leaders to step back from the day-to-day interactions and realize the magnitude and importance of their tasks.

♦ Urban school leaders must understand the importance of political interactions and hold politicians accountable for their role and involvement in helping urban schools become successful. In addition, financial resources should be allocated to those communities that are most desperate.

♦ Urban school leaders should avoid all political interactions that harm urban children. Specifically, urban school leaders should avoid those political situations which require segments of the community to suffer in any disproportionate manner.

♦ Urban school leaders must be open to new ways of looking at organizational effectiveness. Change in urban schools will require a new way of thinking and behaving. Real progress will require collaboration and interaction by teachers' unions, school boards, and community members.

♦ Urban leaders must reestablish their commitment to urban communities. This commitment may come in the form of walking in the community in which you serve, buying goods in the community although you may not live there, and participating and appreciating the cultural diversity within the community.

♦ Urban schools should create "vision teams." These teams would have representatives from all segments of the community and the task would be to create and maintain a strategic plan for urban schools. The vision plans would be shared with stakeholders that could reinforce and financially support the activities. Once again, the emphasis is on collaboration.

♦ Effective community coalitions should be established to ensure that school officials are consistently meeting the expectations of the urban community. These coalitions would ensure that effective instruction takes place in the classroom and that teachers and administrators are held accountable each day for their assigned tasks and responsibilities.

REFERENCES

Adams, L.B. (1993, May). How one school builds self-esteem in students and serves community. *Middle School Journal*, 53-55.

Aronson, J.Z. (1996). How schools can recruit hard-to-reach parents. *Educational Leadership*, 53(7), 58-60.

Atherley, C.A. (1990). The effects of academic achievement on socio-economic status upon the self-concept in the middle years of schools: A case study. *Educational Research*, 32(3), 224-229.

Bandura, A. (1977). *Social learning theory.* Englewood Cliffs, NJ: Prentice-Hall.

Banks, J.A. (1991). *Teaching strategies for ethnic studies* (5th ed.). Needham Heights, MA: Allyn & Bacon.

Banks, J. (1994). *An introduction to multicultural education.* Boston: Allyn & Bacon.

Banks, C. and McGee Banks, C.A. (1997). *Multicultural education: Issues and perspectives* (3rd ed.). Needham Heights, MA: Allyn & Bacon.

Banner, D.K. and Gagne, T.E. (1995). *Designing effective organizations: Traditional & transformational views.* Thousand Oaks, CA: Sage.

Battle, J. (1987). Relationship between self-esteem and depression among children. *Psychology Reports*, 60(3), 1187-1190.

Bausch, J.P. (1990, Summer). The transparent school: A partnership for parent involvement. *Educational Horizon*, 187-189.

Beane, J. A. (1991, September). Sorting out the self-esteem controversy. *Educational Leadership*, 14, 25-30.

Bell, S. (1991). Self-esteem and nonsense. *The American School Board Journal*, 18, 27-30.

Bennett, D.A. (1991, April). Big-city blues: Why do so few school leaders want to take on the urban superintendency? *The American School Board Journal*, 22-24, 43.

Black, S. (1991, June). Self-esteem sense and nonsense. *The American School Board Journal*, 18, 27-30.

Bloom, B. (1980). Early learning in the home. In B. Bloom (ed.), *All our children learning* (pp. 67-88). New York: McGraw-Hill.

Blount, J.M. (1995). The politics of sex as a category of analysis in the history of educational administration. In B.J. Irby and G. Brown (eds.), *Women as school executives: Voices and vision* (pp. 1-5). Huntsville, TX: Sam Houston Press.

Bolman, L.G., and Deal, T.E . (1994). Looking for leadership: Another search party's report. *Educational Administration Quarterly, 30*(1), 77-96.

Bossert, S.T., Dwyer, D.C., Rowan, B., and Lee, G.V. (1982, Summer). The instructional management role of the principal. *Educational Administration Quarterly, 18*(3), 34-64.

Bowman, P., and Howard, C. (1985). Race related socialization, motivation, and academic achievement. *Journal of American Academy of Child Psychiatry, 13,* 134-141.

Brofenbrenner, U. (1976). Is early intervention effective? Facts and principles of early intervention: A summary. In A. Clark and A.B. Clark (eds.), *Early experience: Myth and evidence* (pp. 735-744). New York: The Free Press.

Brookover, W. (1985). Can we make schools effective for minority children? *Journal of Negro Education, 54*(3), 257-268.

Brunner, C. (1994, April). Emancipatory research: Support for women's access to power. Paper presented at the annual meeting of the American Educational Research Association, New Orleans, LA.

Buechler, M. (1997). Charter schools so far. *The Education Digest, 63*(1), 60-63.

Busby, D.A., and Barrett, C.A. (1986). Impact of integrated education on blacks in the South: A participation crisis. *Equity and Excellence, 16,* 57-62.

Campbell, D.W., and Green, D. (1994, January). Defining the leadership roles of school boards in the 21st century. *Phi Delta Kappan,* 391-395.

Cardelle-Elawar, M. (1996, Jan/April). A self-regulating teaching approach to improve minority students' self-esteem in a multicultural classroom environment. *Bilingual Review* 21, 18-23.

Carlin, P.M. (1992). The principal's role in urban school reform. *Education and Urban Society, 25*(1), 45-56.

Charter Schools. (1997). Federal Government. [On-line], http://www.uscharters.org/tech_assist/ta_legal.htm#variation.

Chase, S.E. (1995). *Ambiguous empowerment: The work narratives of women school superintendents.* Amherst: University of Massachusetts Press.

Clark, K.B. (1947). *Racial identification and preference in negro children. Readings in Psychology,* Holt and Co., New York.

Clark, R.M. (1983). *Family life and school achievement: Why poor Black children succeed or fail.* Chicago: University of Chicago Press.

Clark-Stewart, A., Blumenthal, J., and Caldwell, B. (1985, April). *Differences between black and white children during the formative years.* Paper presented at the biennial meeting for Research in Child Development Association, Toronto, Canada.

Clemens-Brower, T.J. (1997, February). Recruiting parents and the community. *Educational Leadership, 54*, 58-60.

Clune, W.H. (1997, May). Building a systemic remedy for educational adequacy: Starting with what we know. *Education and Urban Society, 29*(3), 342-354.

Corcoran, T.B., Walker, L.J., and White, J.L. (1988). *Working in urban schools*. Washington, D.C.: Institute for Educational Leadership.

Cohen, S., and Wills, T.A. (1985). Stress, social support, and the buffering hypothesis. *Psychological Bulletin, 98*, 310-357.

Cole, B. P. (1986, Summer). The black educator: An endangered species. *Journal of Negro Education, 55*, 326-334.

Coleman, J.S. (1966). *Equality of educational opportunity*. Washington, D.C.: U.S. Government Printing Office.

Collins, F. C. (1998). *An investigation of perceived differences in instructional leadership and school climate of African American and Caucasian female principals in Ohio urban schools*. Unpublished Doctoral Dissertation. Bowling Green State University, Bowling Green, Ohio.

Comer, J. (1997). Building schools as communities. *Educational Leadership, 54*(8), 6-10.

Committee on Banking, Housing, and Urban Affairs. United States Senate. One-Hundred Second Congress. March 19, and May 21, 1991. U.S. Government Printing Office. Washington, D.C.

Committee on Banking, Housing, and Urban Affairs. (1991). One Hundred Second Congress, March 19 and May 2. Washington, D.C.: U.S. Government Printing Office.

Cooper, C.C. (1989). Implications of the absence of black teachers/administrators on black youth. *Journal of Negro Education, 57*(3), 123-124.

Council for Exceptional Children. (1994). Statistical profile of special education in the United States, 1994. Supplement to *Teaching Exceptional Children, 26*(3), 1-4.

Crain, R.L., Mahard, R.E., and Narot, R.E. (1982). *Making desegregation work*. Cambridge, MA.: Ballinger Press.

Cronin, J. M. (1992). Reallocating the power of urban school boards. In P.F. First and H.J. Walberg (eds.) *School boards: Changing local control*. Berkeley, CA: McMutchan Publishers.

Cross, T. (1985). Black identity: Rediscovering the distinction between personal identity and reference group orientation. In M. Spencer, B.K. Brookings, and W.R. Allen (Eds.), *Beginnings: The social and effective development of black children*, (pp. 155-173). Hillsdale, NJ: Lawrence Erlbaum Associates.

Crow, G.M., and Glascock (1995, July). Transformational leadership: Attractions of women and minority recruits to the principalship. *Journal of School Leadership, 5*, 356-378.

Cuban, L. (1970). *To make a difference: Teaching in the inner city*. New York: The Free Press.

Cuban, L. (1988). *The managerial imperative and the practice of leadership in schools*. Albany: SUNY Press.

Daniels, H. (1996). The best practice project: Building parent partnerships in Chicago. *Educational Leadership, 53*(7), 38-43.

Danzberger, J.P. (1994, January). Governing the nation's schools: The case for restructuring local school boards. *Phi Delta Kappan*, 367-373.

Danzberger, J.P., and Usdan, M.D. (1994, January). Local education governance: Perspectives on problems and strategies for change. *Phi Delta Kappan*, 366.

Darling-Hammond, L. (1995). Inequality and access to knowledge. In J.A. Banks and C.A.M. Banks (Eds.), *Handbook on Research on Multicultural Education* (pp. 465-483).

Davies, D. (1996). The tenth school. *Principal, 76*(2), 13-15.

Deal, T., and Peterson, K. (1991). *The principal's role in shaping school culture*. Washington, D.C.: U.S. Department of Education, Office of Educational Research and Improvement.

Dent, D. (1989, November). Readin, ritin' & rage. How schools are destroying black boys. *Essence*, 54-61.

Devine, J.A., Plunkett, M., Wright, J.D. (1992). The chronicity of poverty: Evidence from the PSID, 1968-1987. *Social Forces, 70*(3),787-812.

Dodd, A.W. (1998). Parents: Problems or partners. *The High School Magazine, 5*(4), 14-17.

Drory, A. (1993). Perceived political climate and job attitudes. *Organizational Studies, 14*(1), 59-71.

Duncombe, W., Ruggeriero, J., and Yinger, J. (1996). Alternative approaches to measuring the cost of education. In H. Ladd (ed.), *Holding schools accountable: Performance-based reform in education* (pp. 327-356). Washington DC: The Brookings Institute.

Eaton, M. (1997, September). Positive discipline: Fostering the self-esteem of young children. *Young Children, 52*, 43-46.

Edmonds, R. (1979). Effective schools for the urban poor. *Educational Leadership, 37*(1), 15-18, 20.

Edmonds, R. (1980). *Search for effective schools*. Washington D.C.: Horace Mann Learning Center. (ERIC Document Reproduction Service No. ED 212 689).

Edwards, R. (1979). *Contested terrain: The transformation of the workplace in the twentieth century*. New York: Basic Books.

Elish-Piper, L. (1997). Literacy and their lives: Four low-income families enrolled in a summer family literacy program. *Journal of Adolescent & Adult Literacy, 40*(4), 256-268.

Epstein, J.L. (1995). School/family community partnership: Caring for the children we share. *Phi Delta Kappan, 76*(9), 701-712.

Feistritzer, C.E. (1990). *Profile of teachers in the U.S.* Washington, D.C.: National Center for Education Information.

Fenn, L., and Iwanicki, E. (1986). An investigation of the relationship between affective characteristics and student achievement within more and less effective school settings. *Journal of Research and Development in Education, 19*(4), 10-18.

Fenzel, L.M., Magaletta, P.R., and Peyrot, M.F. (1977). The relationship of school strain functioning and self-worth among African American early adolescents. *Psychology in the Schools, 34*(3), 279-288.

Firestone, W.A., and Wilson, B.L. (1985). Using bureaucratic and cultural linkages to improve instruction: The principal's contribution. *Educational Administration Quarterly, 21*(2), 7-30.

Ford, S. (1985). Self-concept and perception of school atmosphere among urban junior high students. *Journal of Negro Education, 54*(1), 319-327.

Fredericks, J. (1992). Ongoing principal development: The route to restructuring urban schools. *Education and Urban Society, 25*(1), 57-70.

Fullan, M. (1993). *Change forces: Probing the depths of educational reform*. New York: Falmer Press.

Gallagher, D.R., Bagin, D., and Kindred, L.W. (1997). *The school and community relations*. Boston, MA: Allyn & Bacon.

Garbarino, J., and Crouter, A. (1978). Defining the community context of parent-child relations: The correlates of child maltreatment. *Child Development, 49*, 604-616.

Gelles, R.J. (1989). Child abuse and violence in single-parent families: Parent absence and economic deprivation. *American Journal of Orthopsychiatry, 59*, 492-501.

Genzen, H. (1993). *A study of leadership style, motivation, and job satisfaction of public school superintendents in Ohio*. Unpublished Doctoral Dissertation, Kent State University, Kent, Ohio.

Gibbs, J.T. (1988). *Young, black, and male in America: An endangered species*. Dover, MA: Auburn House.

Gibbs, J.T., and Huang, L.N. (1989). *People of color*. San Francisco: Jossey Bass.

Gilmore, P. (1985). "Gimme room": School resistance, attitudes, and access to literacy. *Journal of Education, 167*, 111-128.

Glassman, P. (1988). A study of cooperative learning in mathematics, writing, and reading as implemented in third, fourth, and fifth grade classes: A focus upon achievement, attitudes, and self-esteem of males, females, blacks, hispanics, and anglos. Paper presented at the Annual Meeting of the American Educational Research Association. April 5-9, New Orleans, L.A.

Glickman, C. (1998). *Revolutionizing America's schools: The Jossey-Bass Educational Series.* San Francisco, CA: Jossey-Bass

Goodlad, J.I. (1990). *Teachers for our nation's schools.* San Francisco: Jossey-Bass.

Grady, M.L. (1995). Building a network for women in educational administration. In B.J. Irby and G. Brown (eds.), *Women as school executives: Voices and vision* (pp. 131-135).

Grogan, M. (1996). *Voices of women aspiring to the superintendency.* Albany: SUNY Press.

Gullat, D.E. (1997). The parent factor. *The American School Board Journal, 184*(1), 36-39.

Haberman, J. (1991). *Communication and the evolution of society.* Translated with an introduction by T. M. McCarthy. Cambridge, UK: Polity Press.

Hale, J. (1982). *Black children: Their roots, culture, and learning styles.* Provo, UT: Brigham Young University Press.

Hale, J. (1989). *Black children: Their roots, culture, and learning styles* (2nd ed.). Provo, UT: Brigham Young University Press.

Hale, J., and Benson, A. (1989, April 12). Designing instruction for Black children. *Education Week,* 16.

Hallinger, P., and Murphy, J.F. (1987, September). Assessing and developing principal instructional leadership. *Educational Leadership, 8,* 54-61.

Hanson, E.M. (1996). *Educational administration and organizational behavior.* Needham Heights, MA: Allyn & Bacon.

Hare, B.R. (1987). Structured inequality and the endangered status of black youth. *Journal of Negro Education, 56*(1), 100-110.

Hare, B.R., and Castenell, L.A. (1985). No place to run, no place to hide: Comparative status and future prospects of black boys. In M.B. Spencer, B.K. Brookings, and W.R. Allen (Eds), *Beginnings: The social and effective development of black children.* Hillsdale, NJ: Lawrence Erlbaum Associates, (pp.201-214).

Harrington, M. (1962). *The Other America.* Academic Press.

Harrington-Lueker, D. (1993, February). Reconsidering school boards: Researchers and reformers are looking to turn school governance upside down. *The American School Board Journal,* 31-36.

Hashima, P.Y., and Amato, P.R. (1994). Poverty, social support, and parental behavior. *Child Development, 65,* 394-403.

Hechinger, F. (1994). Saving youth from violence. *Carnegie Quarterly, 39*(1), 1-5.

Heckscher, C., and Donnellon, A. (1994). *The post-bureaucratic organization: New perspectives on organizational change.* Thousand Oaks, CA: Sage Publications.

Henderson, A.T. (1987). *The evidence continues to grow: Parent involvement in education.* Columbia, MD: National Committee for Citizens in Education.

Hess, G.A. (1995). *Restructuring urban schools: A Chicago perspective.* New York: Teachers College Press.

Hill, P.T. (1994, January). Reinventing urban public education. *Phi Delta Kappan*, 396-401.

Hilliard, III, A.G. (1990). Limitations of current academic achievement measures. In K. Lomotey (ed.) *Going to school: The African American experience* (135-142). New York: SUNY Press.

Hipp, K.A., and Bredeson, P.V. (1995, March). Exploring connections between teacher efficacy and principals' leadership behavior. *Journal of School Leadership, 5,* 136-150.

Hoge, D.R., Smit, E.K., and Hanson, R. (1990). School experience predicting changes in self-esteem of sixth and seventh grade students. *Journal of Educational Research, 52,* 123-142.

Illmer, S., Snyder, J., Erbaugh, S. and Kurz, K. (1997). Urban educators' perceptions of successful teaching. *Journal of Teacher Education, 48*(5), 379-384.

Irvine, J.J. (1990a). *Black students and school failure.* Westport, CT: Greenwood Press.

Irvine, J. (1990b). Research on teacher-student interactions: Effects of race, gender, and grade level. In J.J. Irvine, *Black students and school failure: Policies, practices, and prescriptions* (pp. 63-86). New York: Praeger.

Jackson, B.L. (1995). *Balancing act: The political role of the urban school superintendent.* Washington, D.C.: Joint Center for Political and Economic Studies.

Jackson, K.R. (1988). Some sociopsychological factors in the prediction of academic success of minority students in desegregated settings. *Dissertation Abstracts International 49,* 2589. University Microfilms No. ADG88-20391.

Jackson May, J. (1997). *The impact of a multicultural racial intervention.* Unpublished doctoral dissertation, Bowling Green State University. Bowling Green, Ohio.

Jackson May, J., and Sanders, E.T.W. (1996). *Multicultural varies that impact preservice teachers.* Paper presented at the Mid-Western Educational Research Association, Chicago, IL.

Jennings, J. (1994). *Understanding the nature of poverty in urban America.* Westport, CT: Praeger.

Jensen, A.R. (1969). How much can we boost IQ and scholastic achievement? *Harvard Educational Review, 39,* 1-123.

Jesse, D. (1996). *Increasing parental involvement: A key to student achievement.* [On-line] http://mcrel.org/products/noteworthy/danj.html

Johnson, F.L., Brookover, W.B., and Farrell, W.C. (1991, April). *Sense of futility: Its significance and correlates among Michigan elementary students.* Paper presented at the American Educational Research Association, Chicago, IL.

Johnson, J.A., Collins, H.W., Dupuis, V.L., and Johansen, J.H. (1995). *Introduction to the foundations of American education.* Boston, MA: Allyn & Bacon.

Jones, D.E., and Sandidge, R.F. (1997). Recruiting and retaining teachers in urban schools. *Education and Urban Society, 29*(2), 197-203.

Jones, K. (1986, May). The black male in jeopardy. *The Crisis, 93*(3), 16-45.

Jones, P.A. (1991, October). Educating black males: Several solutions but no solution. *The Crisis, 98*(5), 12-18.

Kanpol, B., and Yeo, F. (1990, December). Teaching in the inner-city school: The principal's role. *NASSP Bulletin,* 83-87.

Kantor, H., and Brenzel, B. (1992). Urban education and the truly disadvantaged: The historical roots of the contemporary crisis, 1945-1990. *Teachers College Record, 94,* 278-314.

Katz, D., and Kahn, R. (1978). *The social psychology of organizations* (2nd Ed.). New York: John Wiley.

Kelly, D. (1992a, February 20). Separate classes to create equality. *USA Today,* p. 8D.

Kelly, D. (1992b, March 20). No girls allowed class helps black kids excel. *USA Today,* p. 5D.

King, S.H. (1993). The limited presence of African-American teachers. *Review of Educational Research, 63,* 115-149.

Kingery, P., Mirzaee, E., Pruitt, B., and Hurley, R. (1990). *Town and country violence: School safety.* Westlake, CA: National School Safety Center.

Kirby, P.C., and Colbert, R. (1994, January). Principals who empower teachers. *Journal of School Leadership, 4,* 39-50.

Kirst, M.W. (1994, January). A changing context means school board reform. *Phi Delta Kappan,* 378-381.

Knox, P.L. (1988). Disappearing targets? Poverty areas in central cities. *APA Journal,* 501-508.

Kohn, A. (1994), December). The truth about self-esteem. *Phi Delta Kappan,* 272-283.

Kowalski, T. (1995). *Keepers of the flame.* Thousand Oaks, CA: Corwin Press.

Lay, R., and Wakstein (1985). Race, academic achievement and self-concept of ability. *Research in Higher Education, 22*(1), 43-64.

Leithwood, K.A. (1995). *Making schools smarter: A system for monitoring school and district progress*. Thousand Oaks, CA: Corwin Press.

Lempers, J.D., Clark-Lempers, D., and Simons, R.L. (1989). Economic hardship, parenting, and distress in adolescence. *Child Development, 60*, 25-39.

Levine, A. (1990). *Shaping higher education's future: Demographic realities and opportunities, 1990-2000*. San Francisco: Jossey-Bass.

Lezotte, L. (1994). The nexus of instructional leadership and effective schools. *School Administrator, 51*(6), 32-36.

Liem, R., and Liem, J. (1978). Social class and mental illness reconsidered: The role of economic stress and social support. *Journal of Health and Social Behavior, 19*, 139-156.

Lightfoot, S. (1988). *Worlds apart: Relationships between families and schools*. New York: Prentice Hall.

Locke, D.C. (1989, April). Fostering self-esteem of African-American children. *Elementary School Guidance and Counseling, 23*, 254-259.

Lomotey, K. (1990). *Going to school*. Albany, NY: SUNY Press.

Lomotey, K. (1989, December). Cultural diversity in the school: Implications for principals. *NASSP Bulletin*, 81-88.

Lomotey, K. (1990). *Going to school: The African-American experience*. SUNY Press, Buffalo, NY.

Lunenberg, F.C., and Ornstein, A.C. (1991). *Educational administration: Concepts and practices*. Belmont, CA: Wadsworth Press.

Lyons, N.L. (1990, January 18). Homogeneous classes may be best way to curb black male dropout rate. *Black Issues in Higher Education*, 27-30.

Maeroff, G.I. (1993, May). The principal as a team builder. *Principal*, 26-28.

Matthews, D., and Odom, B. (1989, December). Anxiety: A component of self-esteem. *Elementary School Guidance Counseling, 24*, 153-159.

Mboy, M. (1986). Black adolescents: A descriptive study of their self-esteem and academic achievement. *Adolescence, 21*(83), 689-696.

McCarty, H. (1997). Schools can fill the self-esteem gap. *Learning, 25*, 50.

McCloud, B., and McKenzie, F.D. (1994). School boards and superintendents in urban districts. *Phi Delta Kappan, 75*, 384-385.

McKenna, G. (1988, March/April). Our future demands black teachers. *The Black Collegian, 118*, 121-123.

McLeod, J.D., and Shanahan, M.J. (1993). Poverty, parenting, and children's mental health. *American Sociological Review, 58*, 351-366.

McLoyd, V.C. (1990). The impact of economic hardship on black families and children: Psychological distress, parenting, and socioemotional development. *Child Development, 61*, 311-346.

McLoyd, V.C., and Wilson, L. (1991). The strain of living poor: parenting, social support, and child mental health. In A.C. Huston (ed.), *Children in poverty: Child development and public policy* (pp. 105-135). New York: Cambridge University Press.

Merchant, G.J. (1990, April). *Intrinsic motivation, self-perception, and their effect on black urban elementary students.* Paper presented at the annual meeting of the American Educational Research Association, Boston, MA.

Meyer, M., Delargardelle, M., and Middleton, J. (1997). Addressing parent's concerns over curriculum reform. *Educational Leadership 45*(5), 54-57.

Miller, J. A. (1992, September 18). Bush endorses civil rights revisions to permit academies for black males. *Education Week,* 24.

Miron L.F., and Wimpelberg, R.K. (1992). The role of school boards in the governance of education. In , P.F. First and H.J. Walberg (eds.), *School boards: Changing local control*, pp. 151-175.

Montero-Sietero, M. (1989). Restructuring teacher's knowledge for urban settings. *Journal of Negro Education, 58*(3), 332-345.

Moore, S., Laflin, M.T., and Weis, D.L. (1996). The role of cultural norms in self-esteem and drug use relationship. *Adolescence, 31*(123), 523-542.

Morganette, L. (1991, Winter). Good teacher-student relationships: A key element in classroom motivation and management. *Education, 112*, 260-264.

Morrow, L.M. (1995). Family literacy: New perspectives, new practices. In L.M. Morrow (ed.), *Family literacy: Connections in schools and communities* (pp. 5-10). Newark, DE: International Reading Association.

Morrow, L.M., Tracy, D.H., and Maxwell, C. M. (eds.; 1995). *A survey of family literacy in the United States.* Newark, DE: International Reading Association.

Moss, D. (1991, August 13). New chief backs all male schools. *USA Today*, p. 27.

Moyer, B. (1996). Video: *Educating America's Children.*

Myers, S.L. (1991, March 19). *The marginalization of black men.* Testimony prepared for hearing before the Senate Committee on Banking, Housing, and Urban Affairs. Washington, D.C.

National Parent Teacher Association. (1997). *Guidelines for parental involvement: Six steps.* Alexandria, VA.

National School Boards Association Resolutions Beliefs and Policies Constitution and Bylaws. (1997). Alexandria, VA: National School Boards Association.

Neisser, U. (1985). *The school achievement of minority children.* Hillsdale, NJ: Lawrence Erlbaum Associates.

Nelson, J. (1991, May 17-19). Racist or realistic? *USA Today*, pp. 4-7.

Nichols, J. (1996). The effects of cooperative learning on student achievement and motivation in a high school geometry class. *Contemporary Educational Psychology*, 21, 467-476.

Nichols, J.D., and Utesch, W.E. (1998). An alternative learning program: Effects on student motivation and self-esteem. *Journal of Educational Research*, 9(5), 272-278.

Nieto, S. (1992). *Affirming diversity: The sociopolitical context of multicultural education*. New York: Longman.

Obgu, J. (1974). *The next generation: An ethnography of education in an urban neighborhood*. New York: Academic Press.

Obgu, J. (1985). A cultural ethnography of competence among inner-city blacks. In M. Brookins and G. Allen (eds.), *The social and effective development of black children* (pp. 95-117). Hinsdale, NJ: Walters.

Olmedo, I.A. (1997). Challenging old assumptions: Preparing teachers for inner city schools. *Teaching and Teacher Education*, 13(3), 245-258.

Ornstein, A.C., and Levine, D.U. (1990). Class, race, and achievement. *The Education Digest*, 9, 11-14.

Owens, R.G. (1995). *Organizational behavior in education*. Boston, MA: Allyn & Bacon.

Parkay, F.W., Hardcastle-Stanford, B. (1995). *Becoming a teacher*. Boston, MA: Allyn & Bacon.

Parsons, T. (1969). On the concept of political power. In T. Parsons, *Politics and social sciences* (Vol. 12, pp. 536-547). New York: Crowell Collier and Macmillan.

Patterson-Stewart, K., (1999). *Wading through the waters of cross-cultural relationships*. Unpublished manuscript.

Pederson, P., and Carey, J.C. (1994). *Multicultural counseling in schools: A practical handbook*. Boston, MA: Allyn and Bacon Publisher.

Perel, W.M., and Vairo, P.D. (1969). *Urban education: Problems and prospects*. New York: David McKay Company, Inc.

Peterson, C., and Austin, J.T. (1985). Review of Coopersmith self-esteem inventories. In J.V. Mitchell, Jr. (ed.), *The Ninth Mental Measurement Yearbook*, 2, 396. Lincoln, NE: The University of Nebraska.

Peterson, K.D., Bennet, B., and Sherman, D. (1991). Themes of uncommonly successful teachers of at-risk students. *Urban Education*, 26(2), 176-194.

Pigford, A., and Tonnsen, S. (1993). *Women in school leadership*. Lancaster, PA: Technomic.

Pink, W.T. (1992). The politics of reforming urban schools. *Education and Urban Society, 25*(1), 96-113.

Pink, W.T., and Hyde, A. (1992). *Effective staff development for school change*. Norwood, NJ: Ablex.

Pipho, C. (1995, October). Urban schools problems and solutions. *Phi Delta Kappan*, 102-103.

Plank, D.N., Scotch, R.K., and Gamble, J.L. (1996, February). Rethinking progressive school reform: Organizational dynamics and educational change. *American Journal of Education, 104*, 79-102.

Pollard, D.S. (1989). Against the odds: A profile of academic achievers from the urban underclass. *The Journal of Negro Education, 58*(3), 297-308.

Powell, G.J. (1982). Self-concept in white and black children. In C.B. Willie, B.M. Kramer, and B.S. Brown (eds.), *Racism and mental health* (pp. 19-37). Pittsburgh, PA: University of Pittsburgh Press.

Radke, M.J., Sutherland, J., and Rosenberg, P. (1960). children's perceptions of the social roles of negroes and whites. *Journal of Psychology, 29*, 3-33.

Raisch, C.D., and Rogus, J.F. (1995, May). Helping the troubled principal: The central office's formal role in boosting marginal performers. *The School Administrator*, 12-15.

Ramseur, H.P. (1991). Psychologically healthy black adults. In R.L Jones (Ed.), *Black Psychology* (pp. 125-147, 369). Berkley, CA: Cobb and Henry.

Ravitch, D. (1983). *The troubled crusade: American education 1945-1980*. New York: Basic Books.

Revere, A. (1986). A description of black female school superintendent. Paper presented at the

Rodgers, H.R., Jr. (1986). *Poor women, poor families: The economic plight of America's female-headed households*. Armonk, NY: M. E. Sharpe.

Rosener, J.B. (1995). *America's competitive secret: Utilizing women as a management strategy*. New York: Oxford University Press.

Russo, C.J. (1992). The legal status of school boards in the intergovernmental system. In P.F. First and H.J. Walberg (eds.), *School boards: changing local control* (pp. 3-18). Berkeley, CA: McCutchan Publishing Corporation.

Russo, C.J., and Talbert-Johnson, C. (1997). The overrepresentation of African-American children in special education. *Education and Urban Society, 29*(2), 136-148.

Sanders, E.T.W. (1992). *An analysis of intellectual achievement responsibility, attitude toward school, and self-esteem of African American males* as compared to African American males in a traditional and nontraditional urban elementary school. Dissertation Abstracts.

Sanders, E.T.W. (1996). The survival of urban education: Critical issues expressed by deputy superintendents of urban schools. *Focus on Learning, 1*(2), 26-49

Sanders, E.T.W., and Jackson May, J. (1997). *Business firms or superintendents: Issues for urban school superintendents.* Paper presented at the American Association of School Administrators Conference, Orlando, FL.

Sanders, E.T.W., and Reed, P.L. (1995). An investigation of the possible effects of an immersion as compared to a traditional program for African-American males. *Urban Education, 30*(1), 93-112.

Sanders, E.T.W., Jackson May, J., Patterson-Stewart, K.P., Ludwig, R., Plummer, J., and Salazar-Valentine, M. (1998). Outsourcing the superintendency: Challenges to the urban superintendency. *American Secondary Education, 27*(1), 1-8.

Schurr, S.L. (1992, April). Proven ways to involve parents. *The Education Digest,* 4-8.

Schwartz, F. (1996). Why many new teachers are unprepared to teach in New York City schools. *Phi Delta Kappan, 78*(1), 82-84.

Scott, C.G., Murray, G.C., Mertens, C., and Dustin, E.R. (1996). Student self-esteem and the school system: Perceptions and implications. *The Journal of Educational Research, 89*(5), 286-293.

Shakeshaft, C. (1989). *Women in educational administration.* Newbury Park, CA: Sage.

Slaughter, D.T., and Epps, E.G. (1987). The home environment and academic achievement of black american children and youth: An overview. *Journal of Negro Education 56* (1), 3-20.

Smith, W., and Chunn, E. (1989). *Black education: A quest for equality and excellence.* New Brunswick, NJ: Transaction Publishers.

Sowell, T. (1986). *Education: Assumptions versus history.* Stanford, CA: Honover Institution Press.

Steller, A.W. and Lambert, W.K. (1996, January). Advanced placement: Helping to achieve systemwide reform in urban schools. *NASSP Bulletin, 80,* 96-10.

Strickland, D.S. (1994, September). Educating African-American learners at-risk: Finding a better way. *Language Arts, 71,* 328-335.

Stratus, M., Gelles, R. and Steinmetz. (1980). *Behind closed doors: Violence in the American family.* Garden City, NY: Doubleday.

Swick, K.J. and Broadway, F. (1997). Parental efficacy and successful involvement. *Journal of Instructional Psychology, 24*(1), 69-75.

Sylwester, R. (1977). The neurobiology of self-esteem and aggression. *Educational Leadership, 54,* 75--79.

Tallerico, M. Burstyn, J.N. and Poole, W. (1993). *Gender and politics at work: Why women exit the superintendency*. Fairfax, VA: National Policy Board for Educational Administration.

Tatum, B.D. (1992). Talking about race, learning about racism: The application of racial identity development theory in the classroom. *Harvard Educational Review, 62*(1), 1-24.

Taylor, M.C. (1989). Bad boys and school suspension: Public policy implications for black males. *Sociological Inquiry, 56*, 498-506.

Thernstrom, A. (1991, December 16). The limits of racial role models: Beyond the pale. *The New Republic*, 22-23.

Tyack, D.B. and Strober, M.H. (1981). Jobs and gender. A history of the structuring of educational employment by sex. In P.A. Schmuck, W. Charters, Jr., and R.O. Carlson (eds.), *Educational policy and management: Sex differentials* (pp. 133-151). New York: Academic Press.

U.S. Advisory Board on Child Abuse and Neglect. (1990). *Child abuse and neglect: Critical first steps in response to a national emergency*. Washington, D.C.: Government Printing Office.

U.S. Bureau of Census. (1986). *Estimates of poverty including the value of cash benefits*. Technical Paper, No. 57 (Washington, D.C.: U.S. G.P.O., 1987).

Voyer, J.J. (1994). Coercive organizational politics and organizational outcomes: An interpretive study. *Organizational Science 5*(1), 72-85.

Wadsworth, D. (1997). The publics view of public schools. *Educational Leadership, 54*(5), 44-47.

Walker, E.M., and Madhere, S. (1987, April). Multiple retentions: Some consequences for the cognitive and effective maturatioin of minority elementary students. *Urban Education* (167), 85-102.

Warshaw, M. (1986, September). Return from the tower. *Phi Delta Kappan*, 67-69.

Waxman, H.C. (1989, Winter). Urban black and Hispanic elementary school students' perception of classroom instruction. *Journal of Research and Development in Education, 22*, 57-61.

West, C. (1992). *Race Matters*. Boston, MA: Beacon Press.

White, J.L., and Parham, T. (1984). *The psychology of blacks*. Englewood Cliffs, NJ: Prentice-Hall.

Wiedmer, T. (1996). Practice in public elementary and secondary schools. In T.J. Kowalski (ed.), *Public relations in educational organizations: Practice in an age of information and reform*. Englewood Cliffs, NJ: Merrill-Prentice Hall.

Williams, H.S., and Leonard, R. (1989, March). *Self-concept report differences between at-risk and not at-risk African-American elementary students: Implications for teachers, counselors, and principals*. Paper presented at the annual meeting of the American Educational Research Association, San Francisco, CA.

Williams, T.R. (1972). *Introduction to socialization: Human culture transmitted*. New York: Harper & Row.

Willie, C.V. (1985). The problems of standardized testing in a free and pluralistic society. *Phi Delta Kappan, 66*(9), 626-628.

Wilson, F.C. (1989). Equity in education: A low priority in the school reform movement. *Urban Education Review, 9*(1), 16-23.

Wilson, W.J. (1987). *The truly disadvantaged*. Chicago: University of Chicago Press.

Wolock, I., and Horowitz, B. (1979). Child maltreatment and material deprivation among AFDC-recipient families. *Social Service Review, 53*, 175-194.

Wood, P.C., Hillman, S.B., and Sawilowsky, S.S. (1996). Locus of control, self-concept, and self-esteem among at-risk African American adolescents. *Adolescence, 31*(123), 597-604.

Yukl, G. and Falbe, C.M. (1990). Influence tactics and objectives in upward, downward, and lateral influence attempts. *Journal of Applied Psychology, 75*, 133.

INDEX